Contents

Indian
Kitchen

• • • • • • • • • • • • • • •

Indian
Kitchen

Maunika Gowardhan

HODDER &
STOUGHTON

• • • • • • • • • • • • • •

INTRODUCTION...   The sound of chillies spluttering in hot oil,
the warmth of roasting spices, the fragrant rubs
on marinating meats, and simmering curries; all
sounds and smells that tease our senses in an
everyday Indian kitchen.

They could not be more familiar to me. I grew up
on Indian food in the bustling city of Mumbai,
watching my mother and my grandmother cook meals
full of flavour as part of our daily repertoire.
Family and friends all cooking and sharing in the
diverse regional variety of Indian food. Every
dish we cooked was symbolic: of an occasion to
be celebrated with loved ones, especially those
marking festivals of Diwali or Holi; or of a mood,
an emotion that affected what we felt like eating.
Now that I live in Britain I cook the very same
curries and reminisce about the food and emotions
of Mumbai.

Sharing hearty meals over lively conversations
with my family laid the foundation of my approach
to good food. I went shopping with Mum and Dad
regularly — watching them haggle for a few rupees
and finally securing a good bargain came with a
real sense of achievement. I would proudly hold
the basket and walk with Mum. When we got home
we'd sort out the week's shopping while she
planned what to cook.

Some days she would rustle up something quick
for those busy times and a simple Tadka Dal and
rice was as delicious as anything — topped with
homemade ghee and some 'papad' (what you might
call poppadum) and pickle on the side. There were
many evenings like that and we relished every
minute of it as I do today.

Sometimes as a special treat we would have 'chaat'
(street food) themed nights at home. Replicating
street food was probably Mum's way of getting
us to stop eating roadside chaat or 'junk food'
as she would call it — Mumbai Frankie Rolls,
Dabeli and Makai Butta to name just a few. They
were supremely delicious and despite scoffing it
all at home I would still spend days visiting
local street vendors with friends. Many a monsoon
evening has been spent standing under a little
shack away from the pouring rain watching the
street vendor cooking the 'butta' (corn) over hot
coals and then slathering it in chilli, lime and
salt. That damp chill in the air perked up with
every bite of the Makai Butta. These make up some
of my fondest memories.

It wasn't all paper-wrapped snacks on street corners. If you wanted a definition of 'lavish feast' then my home was the place to find it. My mother always played the ultimate hostess, making an indelible impression by cooking a lavish Indian feast when family and friends came over. Without realising it, when I too started cooking and entertaining I followed exactly what she would do: plenty of snacks to go with the drinks, generous portions of curries with flat breads, raitas and also some side dishes — and of course rice was always an imperative part of the meal. Followed at a leisurely pace by something 'meetha' (sweet)! And then finally Adrak Chai to finish it all off. When your guests ask for the recipe or a doggie bag you know you're onto a winner!

When visiting my cousin in Mumbai recently she offered us eight different starters and light bites to go with drinks for just a small group of us — that's before she served the main meal. Yes, that's exactly what we call a feast and I suppose it runs in the family! It started with my grandmother, who was an amazing host. The sheer splendour of a dinner party at her house had to be seen to be believed. My mother always fondly told me stories of the food, drinks — and more food — consumed. The variety, opulence and effort with which the meal was put together made an invitation to a dinner party at her house one to vie for.

Mum's view towards cooking and feeding the family was simple, yet there was always variety. It's the sheer diversity of recipes she cooked and introduced my palate to as a child that makes me more experimental and inquisitive. It's part of my DNA and nothing gives me more pleasure than feeding a crowd of curry lovers some finger lickin' food with an array of gravy dishes, kebabs, chaat, biryanis and Indian puddings!

I have been fortunate to sample some of the best restaurant, street and home-cooked food across India. I have used these influences to showcase the food of the Indian subcontinent in my work as a private chef in the UK, Europe, the Middle East and India. As well as travelling for my work, I am a mum to my six-year-old son. So with a family and busy working life I'm always striving to give the best to both aspects of my life. I yearn to share fantastic food in the process and always ensure that the menus at my cookery events and classes offer something that people will take back and be

able to replicate, but also showcase the essence
of what Indian cooking is really about. Flavour,
spice and regional variety all come to mind when I
think back on the food I have eaten, and it's this
slice of amazing India that drives me to help make
people enthusiastic as I am. And as a wife and
mother I wouldn't be doing justice to my heritage
if I can't share it at home with my family.
Cooking at home comes from the heart and that's
where it all begins for me; getting the family to
savour every bite of the meal we eat brings me
sheer joy.

Travelling the length and breadth of India for
work allows me to explore the diversity of the
country and to soak in all the delectable choices
on offer as well as understand the flavours and
cooking methods unique to various cultures. Every
20-30 miles the cuisine changes — due to the
climate, the crops being grown within the local
communities and of course cultural habits. Even
today, delving into spices and regional flavours
takes me by surprise and excites me, so I stock up
on the recipes. I think that sharing what I know
is a way of keeping these traditions, cultures
and classics alive for future generations which
they can carry forward. And that is why this book
includes wonderful recipes from all over India.

I know that cooking Indian food can sometimes seem
intimidating. So in this book, as in my cookery
classes, I strive to share the secrets of an
Indian Kitchen and demystify the recipes so that
anyone can cook a gorgeous curry.

I'm often asked, 'what do Indians cook on a day to
day basis?' And, 'how is it that you can rustle
up a curry for an everyday meal when you're so
busy?' The answer to those questions is in the
first two chapters of this book. Hungry includes
recipes for when you're starving and short of
time and they are precisely the type of dish
my mother might have made for us on a Tuesday
evening. And Lazy contains recipes for when you
want something a bit slower, a bit comforting,
but still straightforward. Conversely, when you
have the luxury of time and want to put some real
love into a meal at the weekend, you can turn to
Indulgent, or when you have friends and family
coming over then Celebratory is the chapter for
you. And for all the accompaniments you could wish
for — chutneys, rice, raita, bread, spice mixes —
turn to the Extras chapter.

Every dish Indians cook relates to how we feel
— hungry, lazy, indulgent, and the ultimate
celebratory feeling! We associate every curry with
the way we feel on a given day and it felt natural
to divide up the recipes in this way.

Over time I have blended the tradition and
techniques of Indian cooking alongside the culture
in the west to fit in with my contemporary way of
cooking. You can rustle up that mid-week meal to
satisfy your hunger when you're time-pressed yet
keep some really special recipes for occasions
when you feel indulgent. This is the way I cook
and something I have learnt from my family. These
recipes have been a part of my life and nothing
gives me more happiness knowing that it's going to
be part of yours. Knowing that you and your family
will be feasting on my recipe for Malyali Chicken
Biryani or even a slow cooked Chukhandar ka Gosht
— it means I have been able to pass on a little
slice of my life and one that I know will be used
for years to come.

My recipes are simple to follow and there's
something for every occasion, but more than that
I want you to delve into your senses. Like most
people I use some recipes for certain days of the
week; it is ultimately about evoking emotions and
how we feel when we tuck into the first bite of
this home cooked Indian meal; one that I hope you
will cherish for years to come.

It has been inspiring to have had the opportunity
to share some of my love of Indian cooking with
some of my own food heroes. Sharing spice tips
and cooking Butter Chicken with Jamie Oliver for
his online cookery channel FoodTube is a personal
highlight (you can see the videos at www.youtube.
com/JamieOliver). I have also hosted supper clubs
and cookery classes at Jamie's cookery school
Recipease, which has allowed me to show that
Indian recipes don't always have to be complicated
and that even Dal can encourage people to start
trying it out at home and cooking from scratch.

Writing this book has been a privilege and it's a
joy to have the space to share with you the spice
blends, the family recipes, and the techniques
which I know most people yearn to find out about.
Tucking into a gorgeous curry with smells wafting
through our homes and beyond, brings simple
pleasures like no other. That is the essence of
every Indian household which comes to life during
meal times and I hope you find that joy too.

Cook's notes

....

Unless otherwise stated:

All recipes serve 4.

All vegetables are washed.

Onions, garlic, carrots, potatoes
and ginger are peeled.

Onions are white.

Eggs are medium.

All oven temperatures are for non-fan ovens.

Indian Kitchen Essentials

Every layer of spice used in Indian cooking adds a different dimension to how the resulting curry will taste. And, despite the prevalence of heat in Indian cooking, it's not always heat we aim for — flavour is just as important. In fact, the flavour comes from a combination of dried spices and fresh ingredients used together. The two complement one another to produce the balance — spicy, sour, sweet, hot and tangy. With this in mind, I've grouped ingredients into two broad categories: dried/storecupboard items and fresh. The lists are not comprehensive — they focus on the essentials that would be stocked in a true Indian kitchen.

Storecupboard and spice guide

The question I often get asked is, 'What essential ingredients do I need to stock?' Hopefully, the information that follows will answer that. All the ingredients listed feature in this book in their different forms and are explained in this guide, so that you can see at a glance which type are most commonly used.

When it comes to ground spices, my rule of thumb is always to add only as much of them as you would salt or pepper. Remember, spices are there to bring warmth, a little heat and a lot of depth and earthy flavour to your cooking, so use them sparingly. Remember, many of them, such as panch puran and chaat masala, are readily available online as well as in stores, and are really good quality, so it's not worth going through all the hassle of making them yourself from scratch. Stored in airtight tins, they have a long shelf-life, and are indispensible alongside other standbys, such as canned tomatoes and coconut milk, and beans and pulses.

AJWAIN SEEDS

Also known as carom, these small seeds have a hot bitter taste with a thyme-like flavour. They work perfectly with Indian breads, fish and fried food. Ajwain is widely available in stores and online.

AMCHOOR (DRY MANGO POWDER)

Made from unripe mangoes, amchoor has a very tart distinctive flavour. It adds acidity and makes a good alternative to lemon juice without the moisture. I like to use it when cooking bhindi (okra) or even parathas. It is also one of the ingredients that bring out the tangy/sour flavour in chaat masala (*see* opposite).

ASAFOETIDA

Also known as hing, this pungent spice is extracted from the sap of a plant in the fennel family and has an onion-like flavour, which makes it useful in curries and a good substitute for garlic and onions. Sold as powder or granules, asafoetida keeps for up to a year. (The powdered form contains rice powder, which prevents it from forming lumps.) This spice is commonly used in curries containing lentils and pulses as it helps to make them more digestible.

BAY LEAF

These aromatic leaves are a common feature of Indian dishes and, although used dry, tend to keep their flavour intact. Indian bay leaves are quite different from the European variety, having an aroma and flavour like cinnamon when cooked, and if you can get hold of them they're well worth trying. If not, use the European variety instead.

BLACK CARDAMOM

With its woody, smoky and intense aroma, black cardamom is one of my favourite spices when cooking with meats, and is also used to flavour curries, dal and tea. Use the pods whole or break them open and use the seeds inside. *See also* Green cardamom.

BLACK/BROWN MUSTARD SEEDS

Also known as rai, dried black/brown mustard seeds are commonly used for tempering, a cooking method in which whole spices are fried in hot oil. They appear in many Gujarati, Marathi, Bengali and south Indian dishes. The seeds are also often ground to a paste, which can be used in dals and curries. *See also* Mustard oil.

BLACK ONION SEEDS

These seeds, also called kalonji in India, and nigella in the UK, come from the fruit of a flower named 'Nigella sativa'. They have a slightly bitter, peppery flavour and are a good addition to curries, pickles and breads. They are often used slightly toasted to release their flavour.

BLACK PEPPERCORNS

Black pepper is an integral spice in Indian food — especially in the south, where it is grown — and is used to add an additional dimension of heat to many dishes. Black peppers are berries that are picked from the vine and come from the same plant that produces white and green peppercorns. The flavour of coarsely crushed black peppercorn is just amazing, particularly in dishes such as Murgh Kali Mirch (see page 134), where I would recommend grinding a fresh batch. I have also used white peppercorns in some recipes — they lend a lovely aroma and flavour, but don't have so much heat as their black counterparts.

CARAWAY SEEDS

Coming from a plant in the parsley family, caraway seeds have a slightly pungent, bitter aniseed flavour, so should be added sparingly. Used in pulaos, rice dishes and even for baking, they are also known to have digestive properties.

CASSIA BARK

This spice is very similar to cinnamon, but with a woodier, thicker bark, and has a really intense, well-rounded flavour. It is a very common feature of Indian cooking, where its earthy flavour is a perfect complement to meat curries and pulaos, as well as in tea and hot chocolate. In my recipes I specify cassia bark rather than cinnamon because I love its slightly sweeter, warmer flavour, but you can use cinnamon sticks instead.

CHAAT MASALA

This spice mix consists of amchoor (dry mango powder, *see* opposite), black pepper, black salt, cumin, dried mint, asafoetida and sugar. Use it generously on fruit, fresh salads, tandoori kebabs and street snacks to perk them up and lend a tang. You can make your own chaat masala but, to be honest, the shop-bought varieties are so good that it's not really worth the time and effort. Look out for them in Asian grocers or online.

CHAPATTI FLOUR

Also known as atta, this wholewheat flour is used in households all over the subcontinent to make chapattis and Indian breads. It is available in large supermarkets, Asian stores and online.

CHILLI POWDER

There are many varieties to choose from and the heat level varies. *See* Kashmiri red chillies.

CLOVES

The aromatic dried flower buds of a tree, cloves have a warm, sweet and peppery flavour that lends itself well to meat dishes and curries. They can be used whole or powdered and have a shelf life of up to a year. You can grind cloves yourself, if necessary, but make sure to use the powder sparingly as the flavour can be quite intense.

COCONUT Many coastal recipes in India use freshly grated coconut, which can be found in Asian supermarkets (although it is usually frozen). A good alternative is dessicated coconut, but if you're using it for a curry paste, it's a good idea to soak it in warm water for a couple of minutes before using, then drain and use as required. Doing this will inject that much-needed moisture to the paste.

COCONUT MILK An integral feature of many curries, canned coconut milk is something that's always worth keeping at hand. More often than not, recipes will call for only a small amount — not worth opening a whole can for. In this case, I opt for coconut milk powder, which can be bought in large supermarkets and online. Just mix a few tablespoons with warm water for the amount of coconut milk required.

CORIANDER SEEDS The small brown seeds of the coriander plant are often dried and used whole in pickles and curries, but can also be ground. Their citrus note, detectable when crushed or dry-fried in a warm pan, is very different from that of fresh coriander leaves (*see* page 21).

CORNFLOUR A finely powdered white starch used as a thickening agent and even as a coating.

CUMIN SEEDS Also known as jeera, cumin seeds are one of the most essential ingredients of Indian cooking. Used whole, they lend their warm nutty flavour and beautiful aroma to steamed rice dishes and curries. Cumin can also be used dry-roasted, coarsely ground or powdered and added to chutneys and breads.

DAL The word 'dal' applies to the many forms of pulses used in Indian cooking. Toor dal (also known as split pigeon peas or arhar dal) is very commonly used in lentil curries. Being thicker than other lentils, it makes the resulting dal creamier. Channa dal (yellow dried split peas) is also used in Indian curries. This particular lentil holds its shape whilst making the curry quite thick, so is perfect when added to recipes such as Lamb Dalcha or hearty lentil curries such as Tadka Dal (*see* page 50 of 136). Masoor dal (split red lentils) is really quick to cook, probably the reason it's one of the most commonly used lentils in Indian cooking. It's often used to make a basic tadka dal or even a south Indian sambar. Urad dal (split black lentils) is also used in snacks and curries. When ground to a flour, it's a key ingredient in dosas.

FENNEL SEEDS   The dried seeds of the fennel herb (Foeniculum vulgare) have a liquorice flavour and are used in many Indian dishes, including pickles and desserts. When gound to a powder, they have an aniseed aroma and a well-rounded flavour that goes well with curries. Fennel seeds are often served after Indian meals to aid digestion, but these are a different type from those used in cooking.

FENUGREEK   The leaves of fresh fenugreek (methi) have a slightly bitter, savoury taste and are commonly eaten as part of a vegetarian diet, along with lentils, potatoes and bread. The dried leaves are also used to flavour curries and pickles, and to complement vegetarian dishes. Fenugreek seeds are angular, slightly pungent and are also used in curries and pickles.

GRAM FLOUR   Also known as besan, this pale yellow, finely ground flour is made from chickpeas. Use it for curries, breads and in batters or as a thickening agent.

GREEN CARDAMOM   Unlike its black counterpart (see page 14), green cardomom is used in sweet as well as savoury dishes. One of the most expensive spices in the world, it is available as whole green pods which encase its black seeds within. The seeds can be freshly gound using a pestle and mortar to add aromatic flavour to desserts and curries. They can also be bought ready-ground, but this form is not as full-flavoured.

JAGGERY   Also known as gud, jaggery is unrefined sugar made from sugar cane. It is used mainly in desserts, but as it is less sweet than its refined counterpart, it also features in breads and curries. Jaggery can vary in colour from pale yellow to dark brown, and is available in block and powdered form. I prefer to buy a block as it imparts a lovely treacle-like stickiness when added to dishes.

KASHMIRI CHILLIES   These mild red chillies come in many forms: fresh, dried or ground. The last of these, also known as deggi mirch, is my favoured chilli powder. It doesn't impart too much heat and is very high in colour, which for me is important in Indian cooking. A good alternative is mild paprika, but if you opt for this, always complement it with a touch of cayenne pepper, as it doesn't have the required heat when used on its own. Kashmiri chillies in all their forms are readily available from Asian grocers, spice shops and online, and I recommend using them wherever recipes require 'dried mild chilli' because, when fried in oil, they impart a deep smoky flavour. Some recipes in this book also use whole dried chillies in marinades, in which case, soak them in warm water for a few minutes before blitzing them to a smooth paste.

KOKUM
The dried skin of the mangosteen fruit, kokum is used in coastal dishes in place of lemon juice or tamarind paste. The dried whole berries are tart, astringent and lend sourness not just to curries but also to drinks. Kokum is widely used in Maharashtrian cooking, and also in Gujarati and southern Indian dishes. Soak it in warm water before use to extract its sour flavour for curries.

MACE
The lace-like covering that surrounds a nutmeg kernel, mace is dried and sold as blade or in ground form. It has a more delicate flavour than nutmeg and is ideally used in fragrant biryanis and spice blends.

MUSTARD OIL
Also known as sarson ka tel, this pungent oil is used by a lot of communities in India, most notably in Bengal and Rajasthan. Its flavour and preserving properties mean that it is a common ingredient in Indian pickles. The thing to remember when using mustard oil in Europe is to heat it to smoking point, then allow it to cool before proceeding to use it as required — this will get rid of any impurities. Mustard oil is available in large supermarkets and Asian stores.

NUTMEG
The large dried kernel of a tree native to Indonesia, nutmeg comes from the same plant as mace, and its warm, spicy aroma is integral to a wide range of sweet and savoury Indian dishes. For the best flavour, always use freshly grated nutmeg rather than using ready-ground.

OIL
See Mustard oil and Vegetable oil.

PANCH PURAN
Also known as panch phoron and Bengali five-spice, this is a unique spice mixture from eastern India. It includes equal quantities of five different seeds — onion, cumin, fennel, fenugreek and mustard — and can be shop-bought.

POMEGRANATE
Known as anardana in India, pomegranate is used in many forms. The seeds may be sun-dried and used whole or ground to impart a sweet, tangy flavour to

kebabs, curries, raitas, chutneys and dals. Also, a thick, treacly syrup called pomegranate molasses is extracted from the inner seeds of the fruit and is commonly used in curries. All forms of pomegranate are available in many delis or online (*see* page 249 for sources).

RICE FLOUR   Made from finely milled rice grains, rice flour is perfect for pancakes or even southern Indian breads. In western India it is also used in batters to give a really crisp coating. Being gluten-free, it's a useful alternative to wheat flour for those who are gluten-intolerant.

ROSE WATER   The lovely perfumed flavour of rose water is used not only in desserts but also to sprinkle over decadent curries and even biryanis. It is available from pharmacies, Asian stores and online.

SAFFRON   The most expensive spice in the world, saffron is the dried strands of the crocus flower. It imparts a really strong flavour and beautiful colour to both savoury and sweet dishes. For the recipes in this book I have always used strands rather than ground saffron, and, more often than not, they need to be soaked for a few minutes in warm water to help release their colour and flavour.

SEMOLINA   A yellow flour made by grinding durum wheat, semolina is very useful when coating food before frying. Always, always use coarse semolina, known as suji, not the fine variety also available.

STAR ANISE   Red-brown in colour and prettily shaped like an eight-pointed star or flower, this dried spice imparts a strong aniseed flavour. It is available whole or ground and is used in many Indian stews and curries.

TAMARIND   The tart, dark brown paste extracted from the pod-like fruit of the tamarind tree is a souring agent, used in curries to add a touch of acidity, while also imparting colour and thickness to the gravy. Tamarind is sold in the form of paste, concentrate and blocks. Most of my recipes specify paste rather than concentrate because the latter has a deeper flavour. However, as even the pastes tend to vary in strength according to brand, some being a lot stronger than others, it's worth tasting what you have bought before you add it. Adjust the quantity as necessary and taste your curry to make sure the tamarind has added the required flavour.

TURMERIC — Also known as haldi, this bright yellow spice from the turmeric plant is used in powdered form. In Indian cooking it adds colour to dishes and is also valued for its antiseptic properties.

VEGETABLE/ SUNFLOWER OIL — Many people assume that ghee (clarified butter) is the favoured fat for Indian cooking, but that is not the case. It is, in fact, used sparingly, an occasional indulgence, and I always recommend using vegetable or sunflower oil instead. These are readily available and, being flavourless and colourless, are ideal when you are preparing dishes that contain many other flavours. Most importantly, though, they have a high smoking point, which is essential when frying spices.

VINEGAR — Commonly used as a souring agent, vinegar is available in many varieties and is used in a wide range of Indian dishes. Malt vinegar is a good option when recipes don't specify any type in particular. In a few of my recipes I have used Goan coconut vinegar, which is made from coconut toddy (palm wine) and matured for a few months in clay pots. It is available from delis, spice shops and online. White wine vinegar can be used instead.

YOGHURT — Most of my recipes use natural yoghurt or Greek yoghurt, but in both cases I always tend to use the full-fat types because they have a richer, creamier texture. When using them in marinades or curries, though, make sure to whisk lightly first to prevent them from splitting (a hazard when they are thick and fatty).

Fresh ingredients

....

As you might imagine, onions, garlic, coriander, chillies and ginger are among the essentials in this list. When it's flavour you're looking for, these are the fresh ingredients to rely on.

CHILLIES

Ranging from mild to very hot, the heat of chillies resides in the seeds and the white membrane. In Indian curries, fresh green chillies are slit open lengthways to flavour the dish and lend a little bit of heat, while still keeping the chilli itself intact. Those preferred in this book are usually green bird's eye chillies. Home-made chilli paste (made by pounding fresh chillies using a pestle and mortar) can be refrigerated and will keep for 4–5 days. Ready-made paste (useful when time is tight) is a handy standby.

CORIANDER

This fresh herb is integral to Indian cooking, being used in curries and also as a garnish. With its lovely aroma and citrus taste, it's easy to see why so many recipes in this book use the stems as well as the leaves.

CURRY LEAVES

Aromatic and at their best when used fresh, curry leaves (karipatta) are an essential part of coastal cooking. Use them whole to flavour oils and curries, or lightly bruised to release their citrus note. Stored in an airtight bag, curry leaves freeze well, but always use them straight from frozen rather than defrosted to avoid discoloration. Dried curry leaves are also available and are brilliant in chutneys and pickles, or as a garnish alongside coriander leaves.

GARLIC

Whole cloves of garlic are used in pickles and sometimes even curries, but more usually chopped, sliced and puréed to a paste that freezes well. Jars of ready-chopped garlic are available from supermarkets and can be a useful back-up.

GINGER

A pungent, knobbly root with pale yellow skin, fresh ginger is often used as a garnish, but may also be sliced, grated or chopped and stirred into curries to add an underlying warmth. The fresh root can also be puréed to a paste that freezes well. These days jars of ready-chopped fresh ginger are available from supermarkets, and are time-savers when you're in a hurry. Powdered ginger is commonly used in Indian dishes and has a distincitve warmth and flavour to it. Stem ginger preserved in sweet syrup is delicious in desserts and cakes.

GREEN MANGOES   Also known as kairi or kacha aam, green or unripe mangoes are commonly used in chutneys, pickles and curries to impart a sour tangy flavour. They are available from many Asian stores and online. Dried mango is ground into a powder called amchoor (see page 14).

LEMONS/LIMES   Indian lemons are very small and have a lovely zesty flavour. In the UK I find that limes have a similar taste and are a perfect substitute in Indian recipes, especially my Nimbu Pani (see page 242), which certainly calls for the extra sharpness of limes. I tend to use lemons only for garnish or if I require a very small amount of acidity.

MINT   Highly valued in Indian cooking for its refreshing flavour and vibrant colour, mint is often used in chutneys, marinades and garnishes.

ONIONS   In this book I generally use white onions for cooking and red onions for salads and garnishes. White onions tend to be more pungent and slightly stronger in flavour, but make a great base for curries as they turn a lovely dark brown colour when fried.

PANEER   Mild, unsalted Indian cottage cheese (paneer) is made from milk curdled with lemon juice or vinegar. White, soft and crumbly, it's very popular in Indian curries, stir-fries and kebabs, especially with vegetarians. Shop-bought paneer is widely available in supermarkets, but you can also easily make it yourself if you prefer (*see* Tip, page 74).

TOMATOES/ TOMATO PURÉE   Tomatoes are wonderfully versatile. They don't just lend a vibrant red colour to dishes, but also thicken gravies and give a certain amount of tang. I have used tomato purée rather than fresh tomatoes in a few recipes as it has a much more concentrated flavour and consistency.

Equipment

....

My recipes don't require a long list of fancy equipment, but the following kitchen tools will help speed things along!

MINI FOOD PROCESSOR/WET GRINDER

I make most Indian spice pastes with the help of a small blender or wet grinder. The key to making a good paste is that it is finely ground so the flavour is robust and concentrated enough to add the required taste to the curry. I find it's always ideal to have a smaller blender as the paste doesn't require too much liquid and is also very smooth once ground down. There are a lot of reasonable priced mini processors/ wet grinders available online and in stores that are worth getting hold of. As an alternative, a hand/ stick blender would be good to. Just make sure to make your paste or chutney in batches to get the required results.

DRY SPICE GRINDER

Some brands sell really good quality dry spice grinder and are worth having to make the fine powder that Indian cooking requires. Garam masala or any such spice blend gives much better flavour when the spices are finely ground, although this can also be done in a coffee grinder as well.

GRATER

I use a coarse grater throughout my recipes, specifically for ginger, which I add as a garnish to some dishes. Although when cooking recipes from the Hungry chapter, using a fine grater for ginger or garlic is great to speed up the process.

PESTLE AND MORTAR

In this book I use a pestle and mortar when I crush spices or fresh ingredients to a coarse powder or paste, as I do in my own kitchen. For dry spices such as cumin or green cardamom this kitchen equipment is ideal as the quantity required is fairly small.

Recipe index

....

This list is an at-a-glance guide to some of the
recipes in the book divided up by ingredient so that
you can easily find the right recipe for what you
have in your fridge or cupboard! You will also find a
full index on page 250.

BREAD

Bread Pakoda (Deep-fried potato sandwiches) 120–1
Mumbai Sandwich 78
Dabeli (Spiced Gujarati potato sandwich with
  tamarind and coconut) 119

CHICKEN

Achari Murgh (Chicken with tomato and pickling
  spices) 133
Bengali Murgir Jhol (Chicken curry with mustard,
  chilli and ginger) 58–9
Chicken Ishtew (South Indian chicken and coconut
  stew) 143
Chicken Rezala (Chicken in yoghurt, cardamom and
  ginger) 178
Guntur-style Chicken Stir-fry 103
Haraa Masalewala Murgh (Coriander, tamarind and mint
  chicken) 184
Kadhai Chicken Chargha 64
Kandhari Murgh Tikka (Chicken tikka with
  pomegranate molasses) 43
Keralan Kozhi Kuttan (Chicken curry with chillies
  and coconut milk) 140
Khatta Murgh (Chicken with mango and chilli) 63
Malwani Chicken Masala 139
Malyali Kozhi Biryani (Southern Indian chicken
  biryani) 175–6
Murgh Kali Mirch (Black pepper chicken) 134
Murgh Makhani (Butter chicken) 203–4
Murghi na Farcha (Parsi-style chicken with nutmeg
  and cumin) 107
Tandoori Tangri Kebab (Chicken legs with chilli and
  cheese marinade) 82

EGGS

Andhra egg curry 36
Anda Bhurji (Spicy scrambled eggs) 76
Masala omelettes 77

LAMB

Bengali Kosha Mangsho (Marinated lamb curry with
  mustard, yoghurt and spices) 149
Bohra-style Fried Lamb Chops 98
Chukhandar ka Gosht (Beetroot and lamb curry) 144
Laal Maas (Rajasthani Lamb Curry) 196–7
Lamb Dalcha (Lamb and lentil stew) 136–7
Kheema Aloo Tikki (Spicy lamb potato cakes) 150–1
Mumbai Frankie Rolls 122
Nalli Gosht (Spiced lamb shanks) 190

HUNGRY

hungry *adj*
having a need
or craving for
food.

On a mid-week mission to feed the family after a long day at work it's all about making something easy, fast and delicious. We all want minimum effort with maximum flavour and these recipes deliver just that. Take as many short cuts as you need to be able to get that plate of food on your dinner table but make sure, as always, that it is super delicious. As a rule of thumb, I always lay emphasis on making sure to have all your ingredients ready before you start cooking and of course my advice is to stock up on spices that you know you can use on a regular basis. If there is an ingredient that you don't have there is no harm in leaving it out altogether — it might slightly alter the flavour of your resultant curry but you will still have a divine plate of food to thrill the senses!

Grilled, fried, simmered and baked... all make an appearance in this chapter but with really simple recipes. Think GREEN BEAN PORIYAL (page 47), GOAN PRAWN CALDINHO (page 46) or a classic ANHDRA EGG CURRY (page 36) for that bit of mid-week comfort. As much as this section is about something that is simple and quick to rustle up, it also caters for the satisfaction that comes from a hearty sit-down meal you've cooked yourself, despite being famished.

Included in this chapter are recipes from all over India which will show you how different communities rustle up an easy meal. There are vegetarian options and lentils, TADKA DAL (page 50) being the ultimate example, and plenty of chicken and seafood as it's so quick to cook too.

This is how I like to eat when I'm hungry.

All recipes serve 4.

Makai Butta...LIME AND CHILLI CORN

1 heaped tsp Kashmiri
chilli powder or mild
paprika, plus extra
to garnish

2½ tsp salt (sea salt
would be good)

4 corn on the cobs

3 limes, cut into
quarters

How could anyone visit Mumbai and not try
this little beaut! These simple flavours of
corn on the cob rubbed with lime, chilli
and salt are easily replicated at home
(carefully!) over an open flame, or even on
a barbecue. The combination is just what a
sunny summer's day demands.

1. Mix the chilli powder and salt in a bowl and
set aside.

2. Place the cobs over an open flame on a medium
heat (do be careful!). Cook for around 8–9
minutes, turning regularly, until they are
slightly charred and smoky. (You'll know they're
roasting when you hear the kernels popping and
cooking.) Once they are cooked, rest on a plate
for a few seconds.

3. Dip the lime wedges into the chilli powder mix.
Now rub the sweetcorn with the lime, squeezing the
lime so that its juice helps spread the chilli and
salt mix evenly over the sweetcorn.

4. Serve warm, garnished with some extra chilli
powder and lime.

Bhindi Masala...SPICED OKRA WITH MANGO POWDER AND CORIANDER

400g okra

3 tbsp vegetable oil

1 tsp cumin seeds

½ tsp Kashmiri chilli powder or mild paprika

1 tsp ground coriander

½ tsp amchoor (dry mango powder)

salt to taste

FOR THE GARNISH

2 tbsp chopped fresh coriander

1 tsp lemon juice

TIP
......

Apart from lending the required acidity and tang to this dish, the addition of amchoor (dry mango powder) also ensures that the okra stays reasonably dry. If you can't get hold of amchoor, leave it out and add an extra teaspoon of lemon juice before serving.

Okra is so readily available these days that it's definitely worth trying, and this is my favourite way of cooking it. A lot of people are put off from cooking okra because it gets sticky when cooked. The trick, as my mother always told me, is to keep it as dry as possible, by not stirring it too much, and by tossing the okra in dry spices with no added moisture. This recipe is a foolproof way of cooking it for maximum flavour and no stickiness. I promise you it's worth a go. Try it and you'll see!

1. Wipe the okra with kitchen paper to make sure it's completely dry. Top and tail each one and cut into three.

2. Place a wide frying pan over a medium heat and add the oil. When hot, add the cumin seeds and let them sizzle for 10–20 seconds. Add the okra pieces and stir lightly to coat them in the oil. Cover and cook for 1 minute, then remove the lid and give the pan a couple of shakes but don't stir. Put the lid back on and cook for a further 4 minutes.

3. Add the chilli powder and ground coriander; stir briefly and fry, covered, for a couple of minutes, then add the amchoor and salt. Remove from the heat and leave for a few minutes to cool.

4. Garnish with the coriander and lemon juice just before serving.

Prawns Rawa Fry...CRUMB-FRIED PRAWNS
WITH TAMARIND AND CHILLI

12—15 raw tiger prawns, shelled, tails left on

1.5cm piece of fresh root ginger

3 garlic cloves

1 tsp tamarind paste

½ tsp Kashmiri chilli powder or mild paprika

pinch of ground turmeric

vegetable oil for shallow-frying

salt to taste

FOR THE COATING

4 tbsp coarse semolina

2 tbsp rice flour

pinch of Kashmiri chilli powder or mild paprika

One of my best memories of growing up in India has got to be the food my mother cooked for us. Many of her recipes were based on the food she ate when she was young in Mumbai. Living close to the coast meant that seafood was 'in our DNA', as my grandmother used to say. This dish of prawns, marinated in spices then fried in a crumb coating until crisp, was a great favourite with everyone who tried it. Mum would serve it with a dip and some flatbread mid-week, but then she'd pull it out again as a snack with some chilled beers when we had guests over!

1. Butterfly the prawns (see Tip below, or get your fishmonger to do it for you) and set aside.

2. Put the ginger, garlic and tamarind paste in a blender with a couple of tablespoons of water and blitz to a smooth thick paste. Tip this paste into a bowl and add the chilli powder and turmeric along with the salt. Add the prawns to this paste and set aside.

3. To make the coating, mix the semolina, rice flour and chilli powder together, making sure there are no lumps. Now coat each prawn in the semolina mixture, pressing lightly to make sure the coating sticks to the prawns and forms a crisp covering.

4. Heat the oil in a frying pan and add half of the prawns a few at a time. Fry for 1½ minutes on each side until they are pink and cooked. Repeat with the remaining prawns.

5. Drain on kitchen paper and serve immediately with some Mint and Coriander Chutney (see page 225) and a chilled beer.

Photograph overleaf

TIP
......
To butterfly a prawn, score down the body with a sharp knife to expose the black vein. Remove the vein and push the meat apart.

Andhra Egg Curry

2 tbsp vegetable oil

1 heaped tsp black/brown mustard seeds

1 onion (about 110g), finely chopped

2.5cm cassia bark, broken in half

2 green bird's eye chillies, slit lengthways

2 tomatoes (about 180g total weight), roughly chopped

2.5cm piece of fresh root ginger, thinly sliced

½ tsp ground turmeric

½ tsp Kashmiri chilli powder or mild paprika

1 tsp ground coriander

1 tsp tamarind paste

10–15 fresh curry leaves

70ml coconut milk

4 hard-boiled eggs, peeled and halved

salt to taste

fresh coriander to garnish

I've included eggs in quite a few of the recipes in this book because I think they lend themselves so well to curries — when cooked with spices, I promise you nothing could be better! Here a creamy spiced coconut gravy is flavoured with chilli, fresh ginger slivers and curry leaves. Steeping the eggs in the simmering curry to soak up all the flavours really enhances the taste.

1. Place a heavy-based saucepan over a medium heat and add the oil. When hot, add the mustard seeds and let them splutter for a few seconds. Add the onions and fry for 7–10 minutes until they begin to turn light brown.

2. Add the cassia bark and green bird's eye chillies and fry for a further 2 minutes. Add the chopped tomatoes and, stirring to ensure they don't stick to the bottom of the pan, cook for 5–6 minutes until they soften and form a thick gravy.

3. Add most of the sliced ginger (reserving some to garnish) along with the powdered spices and stir for 30–40 seconds or until the oil starts to leave the sides of the pan.

4. Add the tamarind and 150ml water. Bring to a boil and simmer for a minute, then add the curry leaves and coconut milk. Simmer gently and tip in the halved boiled eggs.

5. Let the eggs soak in the spices for 2 minutes and stir gently, making sure the eggs stay intact. Season to taste and garnish with fresh coriander and the remaining ginger. Serve with soft dosas or plain rice.

Masala Mackerel

oil for greasing
4 mackerel fillets
1 tsp lime juice
½ red onion
(about 40g), sliced

FOR THE MARINADE

2 tbsp tomato purée
1 heaped tsp Kashmiri
chilli powder or mild
paprika
3 garlic cloves,
grated
½ tsp coarsely ground
cumin seeds
½ tsp lime zest
juice of ½ lime
1 tbsp vegetable oil
salt to taste

Having lived in a city where coastal food is thriving and the markets are filled with it, it's not surprising that seafood still plays such an important part in my life. In fact, to me, fish and shellfish should be a must for mid-week meals. They are not only really quick to cook, compared to chicken or lamb, but they are also so good for you. Better still, fish and prawns complement spices really well. This masala mackerel is a family recipe based on pan-frying fish in a mixture of spices. Chilli, garlic and lime juice form the traditional basis of the marinade but I have also added some zest for that extra tang.

1. Preheat the grill to medium to high. Grease a baking tray with oil. Score the skin of the mackerel a couple of times.

2. Mix all the marinade ingredients together in a bowl, then spread over the fish on both sides and leave to marinate for 20 minutes.

3. Place the mackerel on the greased baking tray and grill for 7–8 minutes until done. Sprinkle over some lime juice and red onion, and serve with chapattis and salad.

TIP
......
The word 'masala' means 'spice mixture', and it can refer to something dry or, as in this recipe, to something wet, namely the spice marinade. Oily fish, such as mackerel and salmon, stand up well to the spicy flavours.

Photograph overleaf

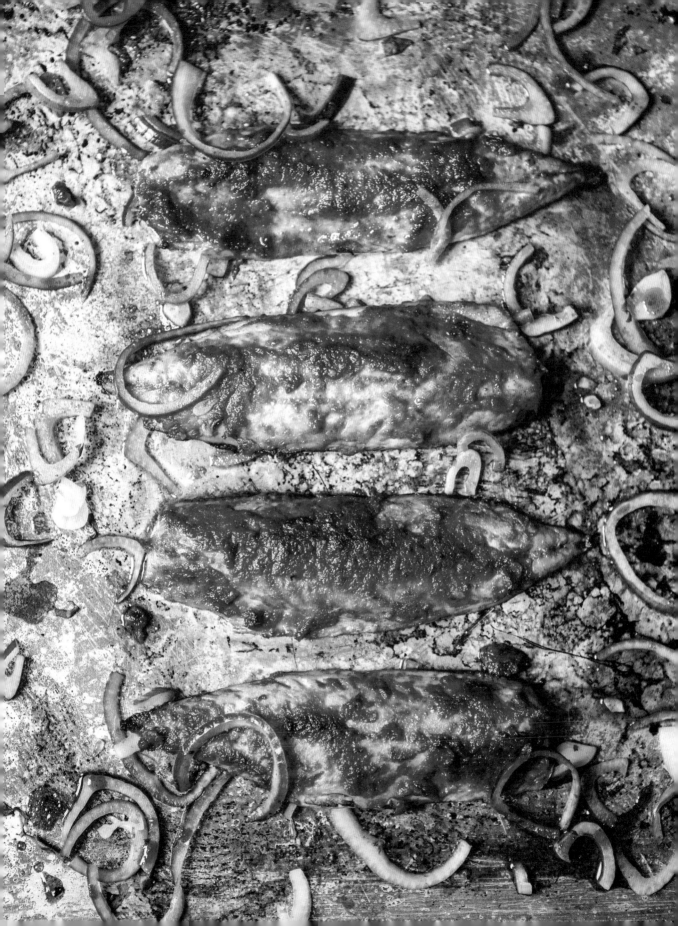

Maharashtrian Rassa...CAULIFLOWER
AND PEA CURRY

2 tbsp vegetable oil

pinch of asafoetida

1 tsp cumin seeds

2 green bird's eye chillies, slit lengthways

10 fresh curry leaves

5 garlic cloves, crushed in a pestle and mortar

1 tomato (about 80g)

2 tbsp tomato purée

1 tbsp jaggery or caster sugar

1 tsp Kashmiri chilli powder or mild paprika

½ tsp ground turmeric

1 tsp ground coriander

1 cauliflower (about 450g), cut into small florets

100g frozen green peas

salt to taste

chopped fresh coriander to garnish

This recipe always reminds me of home, which is probably the main reason why I cook it as often as I do (apart, of course, from the fact that it's really tasty). 'Rassa' in our language means 'gravy', and here a mildly spiced, stew-like gravy is used in combination with the textures of cauliflower and green peas. I find that using the tomatoes on their own doesn't quite give the rich red colour, or even the amount of gravy, required, so I've added some tomato purée to fill those gaps and also to add some thickness. Jaggery is a brilliant addition for that treacly caramelly flavour, but if it's difficult to find, simply replace it with sugar. What you are looking for is a balance of sweet and spicy flavours.

1. Place a heavy-based saucepan over a low heat and add the oil. When hot, add the asafoetida and cumin seeds and fry for 20 seconds to flavour the oil. Add the chillies and curry leaves, stir for a couple of seconds, then add the garlic and fry for 5 seconds.

2. Turn the heat to medium and add the tomato. Fry for 3 minutes or until it begins to soften, then mash it with the back of a spoon and mix well. Add the tomato purée along with the jaggery and fry for a further minute. Add the ground spices and stir well, allowing the raw flavours to cook for a minute.

3. Add the cauliflower florets and stir, then add 500ml water, mix well and season to taste. Bring to a boil and simmer, covered, on a low heat for 15–17 minutes or until the cauliflower is tender, stirring halfway through cooking.

4. Add the peas and simmer for a further 2 minutes. Garnish with coriander and serve this comforting curry with chapattis and Koshimbir salad (see page 236).

Assamese Spiced Potato

1 heaped tsp panch puran (Bengali five-spice mix)

3 tbsp mustard or vegetable oil

1 mild dried chilli, halved

1 red onion (about 100g), thinly sliced

½ tsp ground turmeric

3-4 potatoes (about 450g), cubed

salt to taste

chopped fresh coriander to garnish

India has many diverse regions and I think places like Assam and Orissa have their own unique take on regional food — their flavours and cooking techniques are brilliant. This potato bhaji is tossed in panch puran, a spice mix that's unique to the east of India. The potatoes are fried in spices, chilli and turmeric and the dish is finished off with freshly chopped coriander. Simple, easy and just what we need our mid-week meals to be! I have used mustard oil, which adds a really pungent but beautiful flavour, but feel free to swap this for regular vegetable oil if you prefer.

1. Coarsely crush the panch puran spice mix using a pestle and mortar and set aside.

2. Place a heavy-based saucepan over a medium heat and add the oil. When hot, add the chilli and the crushed panch puran and fry for 10—15 seconds. Add the onion and fry for 6 minutes or until soft.

3. Add the turmeric and fry for a couple of seconds, then add the potatoes and fry for about a minute, making sure the potato chunks are fully coated in the spices. Turn the heat to low, cover, and continue to cook the spiced potatoes for 10—12 minutes or until cooked, stirring from time to time to make sure they don't stick to the pan.

4. Season to taste and sprinkle with chopped coriander.

TIP
......

Make sure the pan is covered when you cook the potatoes in the oil so that steam is created without the addition of any water.

Kandhari Murgh Tikka...CHICKEN TIKKA
WITH POMEGRANATE MOLASSES

6 garlic cloves
1.5cm piece of fresh
root ginger, roughly
chopped
2 tbsp Greek yoghurt
2 tsp gram (chickpea)
flour
1½ tsp Kashmiri
chilli powder or mild
paprika
4 tbsp pomegranate
molasses
1 tbsp dried
pomegranate seeds
½ tsp garam masala
500g skinless,
boneless chicken
breast, cut into
bite-sized pieces
melted butter for
basting
salt to taste

Tart pomegranate molasses with chilli and garlic form the basis of the exceptional marinade in this chicken tikka dish. Spicy, sticky, sweet and tart all at once, it can be cooked over a barbecue for that more-ish charred flavour.

1. Put 3—4 wooden skewers in water and leave them to soak.

2. Put the garlic and ginger in a blender, add a little water and blitz to a smooth paste. Set aside.

3. Put the yoghurt and gram flour into a bowl. Mix well to a thick, paste-like consistency, making sure there are no lumps. Now add the ginger and garlic paste, chilli powder, pomegranate molasses and seeds along with the garam masala and salt.

4. Add the chicken pieces and mix well, making sure they are well coated in the marinade. Leave to marinate for an hour or preferably overnight.

5. When ready to cook, preheat the grill on medium.

6. Thread the chicken pieces onto the pre-soaked skewers and place them on a wire rack. Grill for 7—10 minutes, then turn them over and baste with melted butter. Put them back under the grill for 7 minutes until they are cooked through and slightly charred around the edges.

7. Serve warm with roti or parathas, lemon wedges and an onion salad.

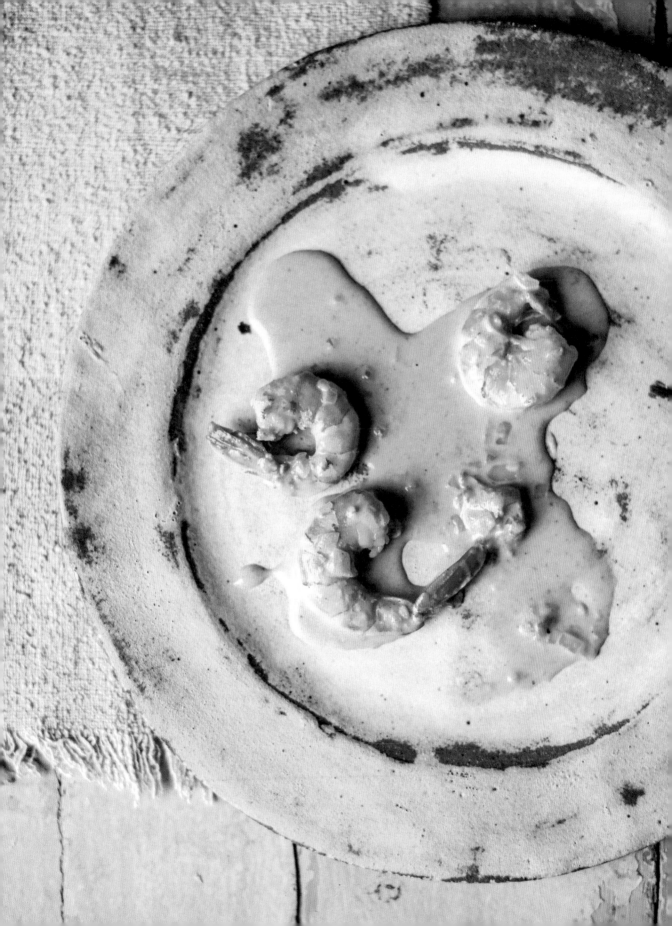

Goan Prawn Caldinho

400g raw king prawns,
shelled and deveined,
tails left on
½ tsp ground turmeric
1 tbsp Goan vinegar
or malt vinegar
1 tsp cumin seeds
15–18 black
peppercorns
1 tbsp coriander
seeds
1 tbsp vegetable oil
1 onion (about 90g),
finely chopped
1 tomato (about 80g),
finely chopped
3 garlic cloves,
pounded to a paste
2.5cm piece of fresh
root ginger, pounded
to a paste
400ml coconut milk
1 tbsp tamarind paste
3 green bird's eye
chillies, slit
lengthways
pinch of sugar
salt to taste
1 tbsp chopped fresh
coriander to garnish

TIP
......
Tamarind paste tends
to vary in strength,
but a tablespoonful
would be the quantity
required of most shop-
bought varieties.
If using a tamarind
concentrate or a
stronger paste, you
will need to reduce
the quantity slightly.

Caldinho is a typical Goan preparation that is mildly spiced. It's usually made with fish, but prawns or even just vegetables are commonly used in the gravy base. It was always one of my favourite curries when growing up in India — my mum often cooked it for the family — but it's also something I have eaten loads of while visiting Goa with friends. The flavours in a caldinho are tangy, sweet and lightly spiced, with a hint of heat from the powdered spices. The slit green bird's eye chillies used at the end add that burst of heat, but you can leave them out if you prefer.

1. Put the prawns in a bowl and sprinkle over the turmeric, vinegar and a pinch of salt. Mix well and set aside for 15–20 minutes while you prepare the curry.

2. Tip the cumin seeds, peppercorns and coriander seeds into a coffee or spice grinder. Blitz to a fine powder and set aside.

3. Place a heavy-based saucepan over a medium heat and add the oil. When hot, add the onions and fry for 5–7 minutes until they start to turn light brown. Add the chopped tomato and fry for 5 minutes until it begins to soften, then add the garlic and ginger pastes and fry for a further minute.

4. Now add the reserved powdered spices and mix everything together. Fry for 2 minutes and add the marinated prawns. Stir well, coating them in the spiced sauce for 20–30 seconds, then add the coconut milk, 80ml water and the tamarind paste.

5. Cover and simmer gently for no more than 4–5 minutes until the prawns turn pink, then add the green bird's eye chillies and sugar. Garnish with coriander leaves and check the seasoning.

6. Serve with Lime and Coriander Rice (see page 234).

Photograph on previous page

Green Bean Poriyal

2 tsp vegetable oil

1 tsp cumin seeds

2 tsp black/brown mustard seeds

1 tsp urad dal, skinned and halved (optional)

1 dried mild red chilli, halved

2 green bird's eye chillies, slit lengthways

18—20 fresh curry leaves

500g green beans, halved

60g freshly grated coconut, or desiccated coconut soaked for 2 minutes in warm water and drained

1 tbsp lemon juice

salt to taste

chopped fresh coriander to garnish

A stir-fry vegetarian dish from Tamil Nadu flavoured with coconut, mustard seeds and chilli. Although any vegetables can be used, green beans are the traditional favourites.

1. Place a pan over a low heat and add the oil. When hot, add the cumin seeds and let them sizzle for a few seconds, then turn up the heat to medium. Add the mustard seeds and fry for 5—7 seconds until they begin to splutter, then, working quickly, add the urad dal, if using, and dried red chilli.

2. As these start to change colour, add the green bird's eye chillies and half the curry leaves. Now stir and add the green beans. Cook, covered, on a medium heat for 10 minutes, stirring a couple of times during cooking.

3. Season to taste and add the coconut. Stir and cook for a further 2 minutes. until the beans are cooked, but still have a bite to them. Add the lemon juice and garnish with coriander and the remaining curry leaves.

4. Serve warm with Curd Rice (see page 233) or even some plain parathas.

TIP
......
I always get people asking me about the best place to buy fresh curry leaves, so I've compiled a list of Asian stores and online suppliers (see page 249). Dried curry leaves can be used instead of fresh, but they have less flavour and, of course, impart no moisture. If you opt to use dried, add them at the end of the cooking time when you garnish with coriander.

Chilli Paneer Fry

280g paneer (Indian cottage cheese), cubed

oil for deep-frying

FOR THE BATTER

2 tbsp rice flour

2 tbsp cornflour

1 tsp Kashmiri chilli powder or mild paprika

½ tsp ground black pepper

1 tsp smooth garlic paste (made from 2 garlic cloves)

FOR THE SAUCE

2 tbsp vegetable oil

4 garlic cloves, finely chopped

1.5cm piece of fresh root ginger, finely chopped

1 red onion (about 70g), cubed

1 red pepper (about 180g), cubed

2 green bird's eye chillies, slit lengthways (deseed if you wish)

2 tbsp shop-bought chilli garlic sauce

2 tbsp tomato ketchup

2 tsp sticky sweet soy sauce, such as kecap manis

2 tsp sugar

salt to taste

2 finely sliced spring onions to garnish

One of the most versatile of Indian ingredients, paneer (Indian cottage cheese) is used here in a dish with Indo-Chinese influences. Such dishes are a regular feature of Indian cuisine and before you ask, no, they have nothing to do with authentic Chinese food in the least! Think robust chillified, garlicky dishes, deep-fried, coated and swimming in thick, luscious gravies. Yes, that's Indian Chinese food and it's more-ish, addictive and so good.

1. Mix all the batter ingredients in a bowl with 40ml water, then toss the paneer cubes in the mixture to coat the pieces evenly.

2. Heat a deep-fat fryer to 170°C or fill a large saucepan or kadhai (deep wok) one-third full of oil and heat until a cube of bread dropped into the hot oil sizzles and turns golden brown in 30 seconds. Fry the paneer in the hot oil in batches for 20—30 seconds or until the cubes have a light brown crisp coating on all sides. Drain on kitchen paper and set aside.

3. To make the sauce, place a saucepan over a medium heat and add the oil, garlic and ginger. Fry for 20 seconds then add the red onion. Sauté for 2 minutes or until it begins to soften, then tip in the red pepper along with the chillies and fry for a couple of minutes.

4. Add the chilli garlic sauce, tomato ketchup and the kecap manis, and stir well. Add the sugar and stir to make sure it dissolves, then add 40ml water to thin out the sauce ever so slightly.

5. Now add the fried paneer cubes, stirring well to make sure that all the pieces are coated evenly in the sauce.

6. Season to taste, garnish with spring onions and serve warm with some Simple Pulao (see page 235) or some plain noodles.

Tadka Dal

160g masoor dal
(split red lentils)

½ tsp ground
turmeric, plus an
extra pinch

2 tbsp vegetable oil

1 tsp black/brown
mustard seeds

1 tsp cumin seeds

10 fresh curry leaves

2 green chillies,
slit lengthways

1 onion (about 100g),
finely chopped

5 small garlic
cloves, finely chopped

2 tomatoes (about
120g total weight),
finely chopped

pinch of sugar

salt to taste

1 tbsp chopped
coriander leaves, to
garnish

Every Indian household has its own tricks
when it comes to making this traditional
lentil dish. My recipe is a 'hand me down'
that's simple, comforting, very delicious and
perfect for when you're low on fresh veg or
meat and pressed for time. Lentils are the
ultimate life-saver!

1. Place a heavy-based saucepan over a medium heat
and add the dal, along with 700ml water and the
½ teaspoon turmeric. Bring to a simmer and cook
for 20—25 minutes, adding a little more water if
you feel the liquid is too thick.

2. Turn off the heat and mash the dal slightly
with a potato masher or the back of a fork so that
it thickens. Cover and leave to cool.

3. Place a separate pan over a medium heat and add
the oil. When hot, add the mustard and cumin seeds
and fry for 20 seconds. Let them splutter, then
add half the curry leaves and the green chillies
followed by the chopped onion. Fry for 4—5 minutes
until the onion begins to soften. Mash the green
chillies slightly to release their seeds, which
will lend a slight heat to the dish.

4. Now add the garlic and continue to fry for
a further 3 minutes. Add the pinch of turmeric
and stir well for a few seconds. Add the chopped
tomatoes and cook for a minute.

5. Add the cooked dal to this mixture, stir and
add the sugar and salt. Simmer for 2 minutes.

6. Garnish with the chopped coriander and
remaining curry leaves and serve warm with
chapatti or rice.

TIP
......
The word 'tadka' refers to the process of frying
seeds or spices in hot oil so that they crackle and
splutter, and infuse the oil with their aroma and
flavour. It's a quick process, so make sure you have
everything to hand before you begin cooking.

Marathi Sweetcorn Aamti...SWEET
AND SOUR CORN CURRY

30g gram (chickpea) flour

3 tbsp jaggery or caster sugar

1 tsp tamarind paste

¼ tsp Kashmiri chilli powder or mild paprika

½ tsp ground turmeric

½ tsp ground coriander

2 tbsp vegetable oil

1 tsp cumin seeds

1 green bird's eye chilli, slit lengthways

6 small corn on the cobs

salt to taste

roughly chopped fresh coriander to garnish

A family recipe for my Maharashtrian corn on the cob curry. It's tangy, hot, sweet and addictive all at once!

1. To make the aamti liquid, mix the flour, jaggery, tamarind, chilli powder, ground spices and 60ml water together in a bowl to form a smooth runny paste. (If it's not smooth enough, pass it through a sieve.) Now add 340ml water, mix well and set aside.

2. Place a heavy-based saucepan over a medium heat and add the oil. When hot, add the cumin seeds and let them sizzle in the pan for 10 seconds, then add the green chilli, allowing the flavour to infuse the oil for a few seconds.

3. Take the pan off the heat and tip in the spiced aamti liquid; mix well to make sure it doesn't stick to the saucepan and return to a low heat, stirring continuously to avoid any lumps. Simmer for 5 minutes, then add the corn cobs. Cover and simmer for a further 5 minutes, stirring halfway through, until the cobs are tender and the sauce has the consistency of a thick soup.

4. Season to taste and garnish with coriander.

TIP
. . . . . .
Gram flour makes a great thickener for sauces and stews, and the effect is enhanced the longer you cook it. If you feel at any point that your sauce is too thick, just add a splash of water.

Patra ni Macchi...PARSI-STYLE STEAMED FISH

2 medium-sized lemon
sole, cleaned and
gutted, or 4 small
cod fillets
1 tsp ground turmeric
pinch of salt
2 tbsp malt vinegar
roughly chopped fresh
coriander to garnish

FOR THE PASTE
1 tbsp vegetable oil
2 spring onions
90g fresh coriander
leaves and stems
50g fresh mint leaves
110g freshly
grated coconut, or
desiccated coconut
soaked for 2 minutes
in warm water and
drained
2 green bird's eye
chillies
3 garlic cloves,
roughly chopped
1 tsp toasted cumin
seeds
3 tbsp lemon juice
2 tsp sugar

TIP
. . . . . .
To bake rather than
steam the foil
parcels, place them in
a baking tray on the
middle shelf of the
oven at 200°C/400°F/
Gas mark 6 for
15 minutes until the
fish is tender and
moist.

Coating fish in a ground coriander and mint paste, as here, is a Parsi speciality. The combination of wrapping the fish and steaming it brings out an amazing flavour. I have used lemon sole as I think flat fish are perfect for wrapping in foil, greaseproof paper or banana leaves (plus, using a slightly smaller one means it will fit in the steamer!), but you can also try it with plaice or simply with some cod steaks.

1. Prepare a steamer. If you don't have one, place a trivet covered with an upturned saucer or lid inside a saucepan of water. Make sure the water doesn't touch the bottom of the trivet. Bring the water to a boil.

2. Place the fish pieces on a plate, sprinkle with the turmeric and salt and set aside.

3. To make the paste, put all the ingredients for it in a food processor or blender, season with salt and blitz until smooth.

4. Place each fish portion on a piece of foil or greaseproof paper (or wrap tightly in a banana leaf) and smear a thick layer of the green spice paste on both sides of the fish. Fold over the edges of the foil and seal on all sides, making little parcels for each piece of fish. (Make sure there is enough room for air to circulate on the inside.)

5. Add the vinegar to the water in the steamer or saucepan and bring back to a boil. Place the fish parcels over the steamer and steam for 12–14 minutes or until cooked (you may have to cook the parcels one at a time if they don't fit).

6. Transfer to a plate, open the parcel and baste the fish with the juices before serving. Garnish with coriander. Rice or Indian bread make the perfect accompaniment.

Keralan Vegetable Avial...CURRY WITH
COCONUT, MUSTARD SEEDS AND GINGER

2 tbsp vegetable oil

1 onion (about 60g), finely chopped

½ tsp ground turmeric

2 carrots (about 200g total weight), cubed

1 potato (about 150g), cubed

200g green beans, cut into thirds

60g frozen green peas

½ tsp coarsely ground black pepper

3 tbsp Greek yoghurt

salt to taste

chopped fresh coriander to garnish

FOR THE COCONUT PASTE

400g freshly grated coconut, or desiccated coconut soaked for 2 minutes in warm water and drained

2.5cm piece of fresh root ginger

½ tsp cumin seeds

1 green bird's eye chilli

FOR THE TADKA

1 tbsp vegetable oil

1 tsp black/brown mustard seeds

1 dried mild chilli, broken

12 fresh curry leaves

A creamy vegetarian curry with grated coconut and many ingredients typical of southern India, including curry leaves, mustard seeds and ginger. This dish has lots of texture and flavour, and a good balance of heat.

1. First make the coconut paste. Put the coconut, ginger, cumin and chilli in a blender with 250ml water and blitz to a smooth paste. Set aside.

2. To make the curry, place a heavy-based saucepan over a medium heat and add the oil. When hot, fry the onion for 5–7 minutes or until it begins to soften. Add the turmeric and fry for a further minute, stirring well. Add the carrots and potatoes, fry for a few seconds, then add 200ml water; cover, simmer and cook for 7 minutes, then add the green beans and cook for a further 8 minutes until all the vegetables are tender.

3. Add the coconut paste to the saucepan along with the green peas and black pepper. Stir and simmer for 2 minutes, then whisk the yoghurt, tip it into the pan and simmer for a further minute. Garnish with coriander.

4. Before serving, make the tadka. Place a small frying pan over a medium heat and add the oil. When hot, add the mustard seeds and fry until they begin to splutter. Turn off the heat and quickly add the chilli and curry leaves.

5. Pour this oil over the Avial and serve with your choice of rice.

Goan Chilli Pork

500g pork tenderloin, cut into bite-sized pieces

2 slices of canned pineapple, roughly crushed (optional)

melted butter for basting

lemon wedges to serve

FOR THE CHILLI TAMARIND MARINADE

½ onion (about 40g), quartered

2 tomatoes (about 150g total weight), halved

4 garlic cloves, skin on

1 tbsp vegetable oil

4 dried Kashmiri chillies, seeds left in

½ tsp ground cumin

1 tsp tamarind paste

½ tsp cayenne pepper or Kashmiri chilli powder

3 tsp soft brown sugar

salt to taste

TIP
......
If you prefer, you can cook the pork in a griddle pan rather than under a grill.

This is my grandmother's recipe, though she used to make it with chicken rather than pork. There is a gorgeous flavour that comes through when you roast tomatoes, garlic and onions to form a thick luscious marinade, and adding the mild Kashmiri chillies gives that fabulous red colour. Slathered over pork, which is then grilled, the result is sublime. This recipe is definitely a keeper! I have used pineapple in the marinade as well — it not only adds a really lovely sweetness to the kebabs, but is also a fantastic tenderiser for meats. You can leave it out if you prefer.

1. Preheat the oven to 200°C/400°F/Gas mark 6. Put 4–5 wooden skewers in water and leave them to soak.

2. Put the pork in a bowl and add the crushed pineapple, if using. Mix and set aside.

3. To make the marinade, put the onion, tomatoes, garlic and oil in a baking tray. Mix well and roast for 20–25 minutes until the vegetables are slightly charred and the garlic is soft.

4. Meanwhile, soak the dried Kashmiri chillies in warm water for 15 minutes.

5. When the onions, tomatoes and garlic are done, and the Kashmiri chillies are ready, place them all in a blender along with the cumin, tamarind paste, cayenne, sugar and salt. Blitz to a thick paste. Tip the mixture into a bowl, add the diced pork and mix well. Cover and leave to marinate for an hour or preferably overnight.

6. When ready to cook, heat the grill to its highest setting.

7. Thread the pork onto the skewers and place on a wire rack. Grill for 4–5 minutes on each side, basting with butter, and turn halfway through the cooking process.

8. Serve with a red onion salad sprinkled with lemon juice.

Bengali Murgir Jhol...CHICKEN CURRY
WITH MUSTARD, CHILLI AND GINGER

3 tbsp Greek yoghurt

½ tsp ground turmeric

pinch of Kashmiri chilli powder or mild paprika

1 tbsp mustard oil (optional — see Tip)

salt to taste

FOR THE CURRY

800g chicken on the bone, skinned and jointed into bite-sized portions (ask your butcher to do this)

3 tbsp vegetable oil

2 bay leaves

3 cloves

2.5cm cassia bark, broken in half

2 mild dried chillies

1 onion (about 80g), thinly sliced

1 tbsp ginger and garlic paste (made from 3 garlic cloves and 1.5cm piece of fresh root ginger)

½ tsp ground turmeric

1 tsp ground coriander

½ tsp mild Kashmiri chilli powder or mild paprika

1 heaped tbsp tomato purée

pinch of sugar

1 potato (about 120g), cut into cubes

130g cauliflower florets

This soul-satisfying Bengali chicken curry made with freshly ground spices is synonymous with eastern India, and, served with plain rice, is the sort of dish that spells comfort food. A nap to follow would be mandatory!

1. Make the marinade by putting the yoghurt, turmeric, chilli powder, mustard oil, if using, and salt into a bowl and mixing well. Add the chicken, mix thoroughly and leave to marinate for 20–30 minutes or preferably overnight.

2. When ready to cook, place a heavy-based saucepan over a medium heat and add the oil. When hot, add the bay leaves, cloves, cassia and the dried chillies and fry for 10 seconds. Add the onion and fry for 8–10 minutes until it begins to change colour, then add the ginger and garlic paste. Stir the mixture well, making sure it doesn't stick to the bottom of the pan, and fry for a further minute to allow all the raw flavours to cook out.

3. Add the turmeric, coriander and chilli powder, and stir for about 20 seconds, adding a splash of water to make sure they don't burn. Now add the tomato purée and mix through.

4. Still over a medium heat, add the chicken pieces and fry for 4–5 minutes to seal, stirring constantly. Add 400ml water, salt and sugar. Bring to a boil and simmer, covered, for 15 minutes.

5. Add the potatoes and cauliflower and simmer for 10 minutes, stirring halfway through the cooking process. With the lid half on, cook for a further 5 minutes until the chicken is cooked and tender and the potato and cauliflower are cooked all the way through.

TO FINISH

2 tsp English mustard
(optional — see Tip)

¼ tsp garam masala

1 tbsp lemon juice
roughly chopped fresh
coriander to garnish

6. To finish the dish, stir in the English mustard, if using, sprinkle with the garam masala and lemon juice, and add a garnish of coriander. Serve with chapattis or rice.

TIP
......

If you are not using mustard oil in the marinade, make sure you add the 2 teaspoons of English mustard at the end of cooking, to lend that required pungency.

Khaman Dhokla...GUJARATI SAVOURY STEAMED CAKE

1 tbsp vegetable oil

1 green bird's eye chilli

5cm piece of fresh root ginger

130g gram (chickpea) flour

2 tbsp coarse semolina

½ tsp ground turmeric

1 tbsp lemon juice

1 tbsp sugar

2 tsp fruit salt (Eno or Andrews)

salt to taste

FOR THE TADKA

2 tbsp vegetable oil

1 heaped tsp black/brown mustard seeds

1 tsp sesame seeds

10–12 fresh curry leaves

1 tsp sugar

50ml warm water

FOR THE GARNISH

1 tbsp freshly grated coconut

chopped fresh coriander

TIP
· · · · · ·
Fizzy fruit salt is best known for settling tummies, but is regularly used in some parts of India for making dhoklas, pancakes and dosas.

This Gujarati savoury cake is made with gram flour and semolina, and is steamed to create a deliciously moist texture. Served with chutneys, it's a perfect snack or side dish.

1. Line an 18cm sandwich/cake tin with baking parchment and grease the sides with a little oil.

2. Pound the chilli and ginger to a coarse paste using a mortar and pestle.

3. Sift the gram flour into a bowl and add the semolina, turmeric, ginger/chilli paste, lemon juice, sugar, salt and oil. Now add 150ml water, a little at a time, to form a thick runny batter. Leave the batter to rest for 5 minutes or so.

4. Prepare a steamer. If you don't have one, place a trivet covered with an upturned saucer or lid inside a saucepan of water. Make sure the water doesn't touch the bottom of the trivet. Bring the water to a boil.

5. Add the fruit salt/Eno to the rested batter and stir well. As it starts to bubble, tip it into the prepared tin. Put the tin in the steamer and steam over a medium heat for 18–20 minutes, until light and fluffy when gently pressed.

6. Set the Dhokla aside to rest for 5 minutes, then run a knife around the inside of the tin and turn the cake out onto a plate. Remove the paper and prick the cake with a toothpick all over to form little holes in readiness for the next step.

7. For the tadka, place a saucepan over a medium heat and add the oil. When hot, add the mustard seeds. Let them splutter for a few seconds, then add the sesame seeds, stirring, until they colour lightly, then add the curry leaves. Turn off the heat, add the sugar and warm water and stir well. Pour the mixture all over the Dhokla, allowing it to soak into the cake for a few minutes.

8. Cut the Dhokla into squares and serve warm, garnished with coconut and coriander, offering some Mint and Coriander Chutney or Tamarind Chutney (see page 225 or 222) on the side.

Parsi Prawns Patia...SPICED PRAWNS
IN TOMATO GRAVY

800g raw tiger prawns, shelled and finely chopped

¼ tsp ground turmeric

1 tsp cumin seeds

1 tsp black/brown mustard seeds

½ tsp black peppercorns

7 garlic cloves

2 tbsp malt vinegar

3 tbsp vegetable oil

1 onion (about 220g), finely chopped

1 tomato (about 100g), finely chopped

1 heaped tbsp tomato purée

½ tsp Kashmiri chilli powder or mild paprika

1 tsp ground coriander

8–10 fresh curry leaves

2 tsp jaggery or sugar

salt to taste

FOR THE GARNISH
2 tbsp chopped fresh coriander

juice of ½ lemon

I am very fond of this recipe. It's something my mother and grandmother cooked for the family and has so many memories that are close to my heart. We always loved eating this with chapattis. It goes perfectly with Tadka Dal (see page 50).

1. Marinate the prawns in a bowl with the turmeric and a pinch of salt. Put the cumin, mustard seeds and black pepper into a grinder and blitz to a coarse paste. Add the garlic and vinegar and blitz again to a thick paste (add a splash of water if needed).

2. Place a saucepan over a medium heat and add the oil. When hot, add the onion and sauté for 8–10 minutes until it begins to soften. Now add the spiced garlic paste and fry for 2 minutes, stirring well to make sure it doesn't stick to the pan.

3. With the heat on medium, add the tomato and the tomato purée and fry for a further 5 minutes until the tomato begins to soften. Add the chilli powder and ground coriander and stir for a further minute. Stir in the curry leaves, then add the prawns. Fry for 2 minutes, then add 50ml water, the jaggery and salt. Mix well and simmer, covered, over a low heat for a further 2 minutes until the prawns are pink and cooked through.

4. Turn off the heat and garnish with the chopped coriander and the lemon juice. Serve with rice and dal or even some chapattis.

Khatta Murgh...CHICKEN WITH MANGO AND CHILLI

5cm piece of fresh root ginger, roughly chopped

7 garlic cloves, roughly chopped

850g chicken on the bone, skinned and jointed (ask your butcher to do this)

½ tsp ground turmeric

3 tbsp vegetable oil

2 green bird's eye chillies, slit lengthways

1 onion (about 180g), thinly sliced

½ tsp Kashmiri chilli powder or mild paprika

1 tsp ground coriander

2 tsp sugar

300g unripe mangoes, peeled and thinly sliced

¼ tsp garam masala

salt to taste

chopped fresh coriander to garnish

The traditional Indian addition of unripe mango to a savoury spiced curry lends a lovely tang to this dish. This recipe is simple and uses readily available spices. Eaten with chapattis and some raita, it's the perfect mid-week fix.

1. Blend the ginger and garlic to a smooth paste in a wet paste grinder or mini food processor. Put the chicken in a bowl and add half the ginger and garlic paste along with the turmeric. Mix well and set aside.

2. Place a heavy-based saucepan over a medium heat and add the oil. When hot, add the green bird's eye chillies. Let them sizzle for a few seconds then add the sliced onions and fry for 9–10 minutes until they soften and begin to change colour. Add the remaining ginger and garlic paste and fry for a further minute, stirring well to make sure it doesn't stick to the bottom.

3. Add the chilli powder and ground coriander and stir well for 20 seconds. Now add the chicken and turn up the heat slightly. Fry the chicken pieces for 3–4 minutes to seal, then season to taste and add the sugar.

4. Now turn the heat to a low setting, cover and let the chicken cook in its juices for 15 minutes, stirring halfway through cooking to make sure it doesn't stick to the bottom of the pan.

5. Add most of the sliced mango and mix well, cooking for a further 7 minutes, again stirring halfway through cooking to make sure the mixture doesn't stick to the bottom of the pan. Now add the garam masala and 2–3 tablespoons water to create a light sauce.

6. Garnish with the remaining sliced mango and the chopped fresh coriander. Turn off the heat and serve warm with chapattis or some parathas and raita.

Kadhai Chicken Chargha

6–8 garlic cloves

2 tbsp Greek yoghurt

1 tsp Kashmiri chilli powder or mild paprika

1 tsp ground coriander

½ tsp ground turmeric

¼ tsp garam masala

700g chicken on the bone, skinned and cut into medium pieces (ask your butcher to do this)

FOR FRYING

2 tbsp vegetable oil

½ tsp cumin seeds

2–3 dried Kashmiri red chillies or mild dried chillies

4 cm piece of fresh root ginger, coarsely grated

salt to taste

FOR THE GARNISH

1 red chilli, thinly sliced

chopped fresh coriander

¼ tsp garam masala

Traditionally a north Indian dish, kadhai chargha is made by frying marinated pieces of chicken in whole spices to form a thick gravy coating all the succulent chicken pieces. This is delicious served with naan and a mint raita or chutney.

1. Put the garlic in a blender, add 1 tablespoon of the yoghurt and blitz to a smooth paste. Tip the paste into a bowl and add the powdered spices. Add the chicken pieces, mix well and leave to marinate for an hour or preferably overnight.

2. When ready to cook, place a wok or a deep frying pan over a low heat and add the vegetable oil. When hot, add the cumin seeds and let them sizzle for 20 seconds, then add the dried chillies and fry for 10 seconds to flavour the oil.

3. Turn up the heat and add the marinated chicken pieces. Fry over a medium heat for 7–8 minutes, stirring continuously. Turn down the heat to low and cook, covered to help create steam in the wok, for a further 20 minutes until the chicken is cooked all the way through and tender.

4. Add the ginger and salt and fry, uncovered, for a further 7–8 minutes to thicken the gravy slightly.

5. Garnish with the sliced chilli, chopped coriander and garam masala while still warm. Mix well and serve with a mint chutney and naan.

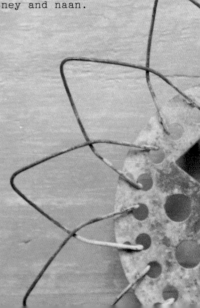

Gujarati Batata Cabbage nu Shaak...SPICED CABBAGE WITH CUMIN AND CORIANDER

2 tbsp vegetable oil

pinch of asafoetida

1 tsp cumin seeds

1 tsp black/brown mustard seeds

10–12 fresh curry leaves

2 green bird's eye chillies, slit lengthways

1 tsp Kashmiri chilli powder or mild paprika

pinch of ground turmeric

1 tsp ground coriander

2 potatoes (about 250g total weight), peeled and cubed

1 white cabbage (about 800g), thinly sliced

pinch of sugar

salt to taste

chopped fresh coriander to garnish

If you ever eat a Gujarati thali, this will probably be one of the dishes included. 'Shaak' means 'vegetable dish', and this one features potatoes and cabbage. What I love about Indian cabbage dishes is that the addition of spices works really well; also, although the cabbage is cooked, it still has a slight bite to it and isn't wilted. Using traditional flavours from the west of India, including curry leaves, mustard seeds, chilli and cumin, this dish is a sheer delight.

1. Place a heavy-based saucepan over a medium heat and add the oil. When hot, add the asafoetida and let it sizzle for a few seconds. Add the cumin seeds and mustard seeds and let them splutter and infuse the oil for 1 minute. Add half the curry leaves and the green bird's eye chillies and stir for 2–3 seconds.

2. Now add the chilli powder, turmeric and coriander and cook for 20 seconds on a low heat, making sure the spices don't catch or burn at the bottom of the pan. Add the potatoes along with 20ml water and mix well. Cover and cook for 4 minutes. Stir halfway through and make sure the potatoes are not sticking to the bottom of the pan. If they are, add another splash of water and cook for a further 3 minutes with the lid on.

3. Now add the cabbage a little at the time, stirring well to mix it with all the spices. Cover and steam for 7 minutes, giving it a stir halfway through the cooking time. Add the sugar, salt and remaining curry leaves.

4. Mix well and serve garnished with fresh coriander.

Easy Coconut Laddoos...SWEET TRUFFLES
WITH COCONUT, CARDAMOM AND ROSE WATER

MAKES AROUND 20

150g freshly grated coconut

150ml condensed milk

½ tsp ground cardamom

2 tbsp desiccated coconut

40g full-fat milk powder

1 tsp rose water (optional)

handful of pistachios, roughly chopped

Here's a Diwali offering that would never go amiss in my household. Mum always made these truffle-like sweets for festive occasions, and I still remember the aromas of roasted coconut and cardamom wafting through our home — I would often sneak into the kitchen, just to get a quick bite of these little morsels of deliciousness. My recipe is based on the way my mother made them, though I do love the addition here of rose water for that beautiful floral note. These laddoos are really easy to make and are even perfect made in advance. They would keep for a few weeks refrigerated. This is one recipe where you really do need fresh coconut.

1. Place a frying pan over a low heat and add the fresh coconut, condensed milk, cardamom, desiccated coconut and milk powder. Fry for 12–14 minutes, stirring constantly, until the mixture starts to thicken and dry out.

2. Add the rose water, if using, and the chopped pistachios. Leave to cool slightly and roll into little truffle-like balls. The laddoos are now ready to serve.

TIP
......
I prefer to use freshly ground cardamom seeds rather than shop-bought powders because just a little is needed and the flavour is so much better. This spice is used in many Indian sweets, and gives a lovely aroma and warmth.

Cardamom and Pistachio Cake

60g ground almonds
150g caster sugar
225g self-raising
flour
seeds from 6–8 green
cardamom pods,
crushed to a powder
1 tsp baking powder
150ml sunflower oil
1 egg
200ml Greek yoghurt
handful of chopped
pistachios

FOR THE SYRUP
100g caster sugar
4 green cardamom pods
1 tsp rose water

FOR THE GARNISH
chopped pistachios
edible glitter
dried rose petals

On Sunday afternoons at home in India, when everything was quiet and the family were having their afternoon siesta, nothing gave me greater pleasure, at the age of 15, than a spot of baking, and making this recipe in particular was not just foolproof, but sheer joy. I was always so proud when I presented it to my parents over their afternoon cup of chai. Fast-forward 20 years and baking hasn't always been my strong point, but there are always some Sunday afternoons to reminisce about my formative years — and this yoghurt and cardamom cake helps me do just that.

1. Preheat the oven to 180°C/350°F/Gas mark 4. Line a 22cm cake tin with greaseproof paper.

2. Sift the ground almonds, sugar, flour, ground cardamom seeds and baking powder into a mixing bowl.

3. Whisk the oil, egg and yoghurt together in a separate bowl. Add this mixture to the dry ingredients, stirring until you have a smooth, thick batter. Add the chopped pistachios.

4. Pour the mixture into the lined cake tin and bake for 45 minutes or until a skewer inserted in the middle comes out clean. Leave to cool slightly while you make the syrup.

5. Heat 100ml water in a saucepan and add the sugar and the cardamom pods. Mix well and simmer over a low heat for 4–5 minutes or until the sugar dissolves. Remove from the heat — the syrup will thicken as it cools. Add the rose water and mix.

6. Transfer the cake to a plate and, using a skewer, prick a few holes in the surface at regular intervals. Pour over the syrup while it is still warm. The cake will soak up the residue from the plate.

7. Garnish with chopped pistachios, edible glitter and dried rose petals. Serve the cake on its own or with some fresh fruit.

LAZY

आलस

lazy *adj*
disinclination
to activity or
exertion despite
having the ability
to do so.

Full of recipes for leisurely meals to be savoured and the most comforting of comfort food, this might be my favourite chapter; from AMRITSARI MACCHI (fried fish with carom seeds, chilli and ginger) on page 106, to a sixty-year-old recipe for MURGHI NA FARCHA (Parsi-style chicken with nutmeg and cumin) on page 107.

Eating a MUMBAI SANDWICH at a street stall, watching as the 'sandwichwalla' stacked up the vegetables, chutney and cheese to make something so simple so very delicious made me think this recipe had to be part of the book, on page 78. You will find other street food delights in this chapter too, inspired by those I was eating from a very young age and always an absolute delight — the ultimate for me are ONION PAKODAS (page 88) which are crisp, full of flavour and just what a lazy day demands, especially with a cup of chai. All these tasty morsels are easily replicated at home and will give you a sense of what gets served across streets in India.

A spicy breakfast such as a MASALA OMELETTE (page 77) or PANEER BHURJI (page 74) is the best way to perk up the weekend. I would not be doing my Maharashtrian family proud if I didn't include BATATE POHE (page 86), one of the main staples if you go to any Mumbai household.

Sit back, relax, and enjoy!

All recipes serve 4.

Paneer Bhurji...STIR-FRIED PANEER WITH CHILLI, TURMERIC AND PEPPERS

290g block of paneer (Indian cottage cheese — see Tip if you want to make your own)

2 tbsp vegetable oil

1 tsp cumin seeds

1 onion (about 90g), finely chopped

4cm piece of fresh root ginger, coarsely grated

3 green bird's eye chillies, finely chopped

1 tsp ground turmeric

1 tomato (about 60g), finely chopped

1 red pepper (about 150g), finely chopped

¼ tsp garam masala

1 tbsp lemon juice

finely chopped fresh coriander

salt to taste

Bhurji is usually a dish of scrambled egg (see page 76), but this version is made with paneer (Indian cottage cheese). It's great for vegetarians, but also makes a fantastic addition to any brunch, or can even be eaten as a tasty snack. Simple to make and super-delicious.

1. Grate the paneer coarsely and set aside.

2. Place a frying pan over a medium heat and add the oil. When hot, add the cumin seeds, fry for a minute, then add the onion and sauté for 7–8 minutes until it softens. Add the ginger and chillies and mix for a minute. Add the turmeric, stir well, then tip in the tomato and cook for about 1 minute or until it begins to soften.

3. Add the red pepper and fry for 2 minutes, then add the grated paneer and mix well. Cover and cook for about 1 minute, then turn off the heat. Add the garam masala and season to taste.

4. Stir in the lemon juice and coriander and serve alongside white toast or even with some naan and chutney.

TIP
. . . . . .
Here's a simple method for making your own paneer. Bring 2 litres of full-fat milk to a boil. Lower the heat to a simmer and add 2 tablespoons of lemon juice. The milk will begin to curdle. Strain the mixture through a muslin-lined sieve. Rinse the curds under running cold water, then gather up the muslin and squeeze out all the moisture. Place the curds, still in the muslin, on a plate and flatten them out a bit. Sit a heavy weight on top and leave to set for 2-3 hours. Cut into bite-sized pieces and use as required.

Anda Bhurji...SPICY SCRAMBLED EGGS

4 eggs
2 tbsp vegetable oil
2 onions (about 120g total weight), finely chopped
2 green bird's eye chillies, chopped
½ tsp ground turmeric
¼ tsp Kashmiri chilli powder or mild paprika
½ tsp ground cumin
2 tomatoes (about 140g total weight), finely chopped
salt to taste

FOR THE GARNISH

2 tbsp finely chopped fresh coriander
2 tsp lemon juice

This gives regular scrambled egg a run for its money. Piled high on crusty sourdough with a drizzle of some hot sauce or rolled in a chapatti, this is a weekend breakfast perked up for sure. However, much as I would like to say it's an ideal breakfast option, nothing tastes better than Anda Bhurji on buttered toast for a late-night food fix!

1. Put the eggs and a pinch of salt in a bowl and beat lightly.

2. Place a non-stick frying pan over a medium heat and add the oil. When hot, add the onions and fry for about 6 minutes or until they soften. Add the chopped bird's eye chillies and fry for a further minute, then add the turmeric, chilli and cumin and fry for a further 30 seconds. Mix well, then add the tomatoes along with the salt and cook for 4 minutes until they begin to soften.

3. Pour the beaten eggs into the pan and leave for 30 seconds before you begin to stir. Cook for 2–3 minutes until scrambled.

4. Garnish with the coriander, sprinkle over some lemon juice and serve warm, piling up the Bhurji on toast or even rolling it in chapattis.

Masala Omelettes

1 tsp cumin seeds
2 green bird's eye chillies
1 onion (about 200g), finely chopped
1 tomato (about 100g), finely chopped
2 tbsp chopped fresh coriander
½ tsp Kashmiri chilli powder or mild paprika
½ tsp ground turmeric
4 eggs
2 tbsp vegetable oil or butter, plus extra for frying
1 tsp lemon juice
salt to taste

This is my 'go to' breakfast — perfect for a lazy weekend. It's what you might call a tarted-up omelette. The way I see it, there's your plain old omelette and then there's this amazing Indian-style masala omelette! The combination of ground spices, chillies and eggs works really well, and reminds me of when Mum would serve this rolled in warm chapattis. Every bite was savoured as I dunked it in some sweet chilli sauce or ketchup. And that's exactly how I like it now. Do increase the amount of chilli if you would like a touch more heat.

1. Pound the cumin seeds and bird's eye chillies to a coarse paste using a pestle and mortar. Place in a mixing bowl along with the chopped onion, tomato, coriander, chilli powder and turmeric. Mix well and season to taste. Break in the eggs and whisk lightly.

2. Place a medium-sized non-stick frying pan over a medium heat and add 2 tablespoons of the oil. When hot, pour a quarter of the egg mixture into the pan, making sure to distribute it evenly. Cook the underside of the omelette for 1—2 minutes until it sets, is light brown and slightly crisp around the edges. Flip the omelette, press lightly with the back of a spatula and cook for another 1—2 minutes. Set aside and keep warm. Repeat this step to make 3 more omelettes, adding a little more oil to the pan as required.

3. Fold over the cooked masala omelettes, sprinkle over a little lemon juice and serve stuffed in bread or rolled up in chapatti. Dunk in sweet chilli sauce, green chutney or tomato ketchup as you eat them.

Mumbai Sandwich

8 slices of soft
white bread
4 tbsp softened
salted butter
1 red onion (about
90g), thinly sliced
1 small cucumber,
thinly sliced
1 potato (about
190g), boiled and
sliced
2 tomatoes (about
200g total weight),
thinly sliced
2 green bird's eye
chillies, finely
chopped
90g Cheddar cheese,
grated, plus extra
for sprinkling
salt to taste

FOR THE SPICE MIX
½ tsp ground cumin
½ tsp ground cinnamon
½ tsp amchoor (dry
mango powder)
½ tsp ground black
pepper
½ tsp salt

FOR THE CHUTNEY
40g fresh mint leaves
40g fresh coriander
leaves and stems
juice of 1 lemon
1 green bird's eye
chilli
1 tomato (about 40g)
1.5cm piece of fresh
root ginger
2 tsp sugar

The iconic Bombay sandwich, which I have eaten over and over again from a really young age yet can never get enough of. The memories are clear...there is a long queue, but it's worth the wait, and once I get there, I go for my 'usual' (with Wibs bread and Amul butter of course — my favourite Indian brands), topped with chutney, tomato, onions and copious amounts of cheese with spices. Delicious! This may seem like a long-winded recipe for a sandwich, but trust me — every bite will give you a taste of what it's like to stand by the street vendors in Mumbai, having a plate (or three!) of them.

1. First make the spice mix. Put all the ingredients for it in a bowl, mix well and set aside.

2. To make the chutney, put all the ingredients into a blender or food processor with a little water and a pinch of salt. Blitz to a fine paste.

3. Pile up the slices of bread and trim off the edges. Make sure you don't take all the crust off — just even out the edges.

4. Arrange the bread on a plate and spread each slice with butter, then the chutney.

5. Top 4 slices with the red onion followed by a generous sprinkle of the spice mix, then a layer of cucumber and potato with a little more of the spice masala mix. Then add some tomato with a sprinkling of the masala mix, and finally the chopped chillies. Top the other 4 slices with the grated cheese and close each sandwich, pressing down lightly.

6. If there is any leftover chutney, spread it on top of the sandwiches. Sprinkle with more cheese. Cut each sandwich into 4 and serve with some extra chutney and ketchup from the recipe.

Upma...SOUTH INDIAN SPICED SEMOLINA

2 tbsp vegetable oil

1 tsp black/brown mustard seeds

10 fresh curry leaves

2 green bird's eye chillies, finely chopped

1 onion (about 70g), finely chopped

½ tsp ground turmeric

2.5cm piece of fresh root ginger, finely chopped

80g fine green beans, chopped

1 carrot (about 80g), finely chopped

260g coarse semolina

salt to taste

chopped fresh coriander to garnish

This is a south Indian snack you will never tire of. I have eaten it at train stations, outside college canteens and at home too, though it always tasted best when shared with friends over piping hot coffee with some gossip at a traditional south Indian coffee house... Nowadays, cooking it at home is usually a weekend thing. Comfort is a bowl of steaming spiced Upma with my cup of chai. With its traditional flavours of curry leaves, mustard seeds and vegetables, this is most definitely my go-to snack.

1. Place a heavy-based pan over a medium heat and add the oil. When hot, add the mustard seeds and curry leaves. Let them splutter for a minute, then add the green chilli and fry for 30 seconds.

2. Add the onions and sauté for 7–8 minutes until softened but not coloured. Add the turmeric and ginger, cooking for a further minute. Tip in the beans and carrots and cook for about 3 minutes until they are half done. Now add 350ml water and bring to a boil. Cook for another 3 minutes or until the vegetables are cooked through.

3. Now add the semolina, a little at a time, working your way through it quickly, and cook for about a minute, stirring well to make sure it's mixed thoroughly. Add the salt and stir — it will form a few lumps but that should be fine.

4. Remove the Upma from the heat and cover, to let the steam work through the semolina. Garnish with coriander, and serve on its own or with some yoghurt, accompanied by a cup of chai.

Tandoori Tangri Kebab...CHICKEN LEGS
WITH CHILLI AND CHEESE MARINADE

juice of 1 lime
1 tsp mild chilli powder
¼ tsp garam masala
10 chicken drumsticks
juice of ½ lemon
salt to taste

FOR THE MARINADE
90g grated Cheddar cheese (you can also mix in some Swiss Gruyère, which will be quite melty and cling to the chicken)
1 heaped tsp cornflour
3 tbsp Greek yoghurt
30ml double cream
1 egg
2 tbsp ginger and garlic paste (made from a 4 cm piece of fresh root ginger and 7 small garlic cloves)
1 tbsp chopped fresh coriander

FOR BASTING
2 tbsp melted butter
1 tsp coarsely ground black pepper

I can't really take credit for this recipe: it's here thanks to my cousin. When I was in Mumbai visiting my family last year, she cooked us a lavish feast with eight different types of snacks and finger foods before we were even served the main course. One of those that stood out was the Tangri Kebabs. She used similar spices to those listed here, except that she also stuffed them with grated paneer, which I have swapped for regular Cheddar. The marinade of cream, grated cheese and garlic is one I often rustle up mid-week and is perfect for chicken.

1. Mix the lime juice, a pinch of salt, chilli powder and garam masala together in a bowl. Score the chicken drumsticks and add them to the bowl. Mix well, then set aside.

2. To make the marinade, put the cheese, cornflour, yoghurt, double cream and egg in a bowl and mix well. Add the ginger and garlic paste, coriander and a pinch of salt.

3. Add the chicken pieces to the marinade one at a time. Make sure to coat them well and push the marinade into the cuts in the chicken. Refrigerate and let the chicken soak in the flavours for 2—3 hours or preferably overnight.

4. When ready to cook, preheat the oven to 180°C/350°F/Gas mark 4.

5. Mix the melted butter with the black pepper. Remove the chicken from the marinade and place it on a wire rack over a baking tray. Cook in the oven for 30—35 minutes or until the chicken is cooked through, making sure to baste with the pepper-butter mix a couple of times during the cooking process.

6. Sprinkle over some lemon juice and serve with Mint and Coriander Chutney (see page 225) and some sliced onions.

Chickpea Sundal...STIR-FRIED SPICY CHICKPEAS

2 tbsp vegetable oil
pinch of asafoetida
1 tsp black/brown
mustard seeds
1 dried red Kashmiri
chilli, or any mild
dried chilli, halved
2 green bird's
eye chillies, slit
lengthways
10—15 fresh or dried
curry leaves
800g canned
chickpeas, drained
and rinsed
2 tbsp freshly grated
or desiccated coconut
1 tbsp lemon juice
salt to taste
1 tbsp chopped fresh
coriander to garnish

For most daily commuters across India, waiting for that train, bus or taxi can only mean snacking on something that will be time well spent. Chickpea Sundal, a stir-fried south Indian snack served at stations and street stalls, fits the bill perfectly. Using curry leaves, mustard seeds and canned chickpeas, it's so quick to rustle up!

1. Place a heavy-based wok or kadhai over a medium heat and add the oil. When hot, add the asafoetida and mustard seeds and fry until they begin to splutter. Add the red chilli, stir for a few seconds, then add the green chilli along with most of the curry leaves (reserve a few to use at the end). Allow to infuse the oil for about 5 seconds.

2. Add the chickpeas, stir for a minute, then add the coconut and mix well. Turn down the heat to low and fry, covered, for a further 4 minutes until the chickpeas have softened and are coated in the spices.

3. Turn off the heat and add the reserved curry leaves, the lemon juice and salt. Garnish with coriander and serve the Sundal warm or cold.

Photograph overleaf

Batate Pohe...FLAKED RICE WITH TURMERIC, CHILLI AND FRESH CORIANDER

350g poha (flattened rice)

2 tbsp vegetable oil

pinch of asafoetida

2 green bird's eye chillies, finely chopped

7–10 fresh curry leaves

½ tsp ground turmeric

1 onion (about 90g), finely chopped

1 potato (about 110g), diced into bite-sized cubes

salt to taste

FOR THE GARNISH

chopped fresh coriander

juice of ½ lemon

In this typical dish from the west of India, flaky dried rice that's been flattened is cooked with turmeric, bird's eye chillies and potatoes. Poha, as it's known, is favoured in Mumbai households as a snack or even at breakfast with chai. It's simple to make and the rice is available in many of the larger supermarkets and Asian shops (see page 249). Try to get hold of the medium or thicker variety of poha as you want it to be fluffy and light rather than sticky when it cooks.

1. Put the poha in a bowl with enough cold water to cover it and soak for 15 minutes to soften. Drain and leave to dry slightly over a sieve while you prepare the rest of the ingredients.

2. Place a large saucepan over a low heat and add the oil. When hot, add the asafoetida along with the bird's eye chillies, curry leaves and turmeric and fry for a few seconds. Add the onion and fry over a medium heat for 6 minutes or until it begins to soften.

3. Now add the potato with 80ml water. Cover and cook for 3–5 minutes on a low heat, stirring halfway through the cooking to make sure the vegetables don't stick to the pan.

4. Once the potatoes are done and the water has evaporated, add the poha. With the heat low, stir well and season. Cook, covered, for 1 minute to make sure the poha soaks in all the flavours.

5. Garnish with coriander and lemon juice and serve warm with a pickle of your choice or even some yoghurt.

Onion Pakode

MAKES AROUND 12 PAKORAS

80g gram (chickpea) flour

2 tbsp coarse semolina

2 onions (about 150g total weight), thinly sliced

1½ tsp coarsely ground cumin seeds

2 green bird's eye chillies, finely chopped

1 tsp coarsely ground fennel seeds

½ tsp ground turmeric

¼ tsp mild chilli powder

3 tbsp finely chopped fresh coriander leaves

oil for deep-frying

salt to taste

There are many versions of this recipe, which you might know as 'bhaji' — mine is all about the flavour and crispy onions with much less batter than usual, making them less stodgy. Always bear in mind when making them that what you're really looking for is more onions and less gram flour. That's where all the flavour is.

1. Put the gram flour and semolina into a small bowl, mix well and set aside.

2. Put the onions, cumin seeds, green chillies, fennel seeds, turmeric, chilli powder and fresh coriander in a separate bowl. Mix well and add the gram flour mixture and some salt. Now slowly add 70ml water a little at a time. The mixture will become quite sticky, but mix well to ensure that the onions are completely coated by the batter.

3. Heat a deep-fat fryer to 170°C or fill a large saucepan or kadhai (deep wok) one-third full of oil and heat until a cube of bread dropped into the hot oil sizzles and turns golden brown in 30 seconds. Drop small spoonfuls of batter into the hot oil and deep-fry for 4—5 minutes until crisp and golden brown. Turn the pakoras a few times in the oil to make sure they colour evenly. Drain on kitchen paper.

4. Serve with a chutney of your choice.

TIPS
......
Making pakoras is really simple, and adding semolina helps keep them light. However, the best way to avoid stodginess is to use the batter straight away rather than letting it sit around for a while.

You can also use this batter recipe to make an aloo (potato) bhajia variation. Just thinly slice 150g potatoes into rounds, dip them in the batter and fry until crisp.

U.P.-style Aloo ki Sabzi
...POTATO CURRY

2 tbsp vegetable oil

pinch of asafoetida

1 tsp cumin seeds

2 green bird's eye chillies, slit lengthways

2.5cm piece of fresh root ginger, finely grated

3–4 potatoes (about 550g total weight), boiled and diced

1 heaped tsp ground coriander

100g frozen green peas

100ml Greek yoghurt

pinch of sugar

salt to taste

chopped fresh coriander to garnish

There is something really comforting about a hearty, mild-flavoured potato curry served with deep-fried puris; this Uttar Pradesh traditional potato curry is exactly that. Eaten at breakfast or any time in the day, it's easy to see why it's so very popular.

1. Place a heavy-based saucepan over a medium heat and add the oil. When hot, add the asafoetida, cumin seeds and bird's eye chillies; let them sizzle and infuse the oil for 7–10 seconds. Now add the grated ginger and fry for a further 5 seconds, stirring to make sure it doesn't stick to the bottom of the pan.

2. Tip in the boiled potatoes along with the ground coriander and stir well over a medium heat. Add 150ml water along with the green peas. Bring to a boil, then simmer on a low heat and add the yoghurt a tablespoon at a time, stirring well. Cover and continue to simmer for 5–6 minutes, stirring halfway through cooking, until the gravy has thickened slightly and forms a creamy consistency.

3. Add the sugar and salt and garnish with chopped coriander. Serve with Puris (see page 227).

TIP
......
I use all-purpose potatoes in this recipe, and boil them before adding them to the curry. This not only shortens the overall cooking time, but the starch from them thickens the gravy, making it the perfect consistency for scooping up with flatbread or puri.

Haraa Paneer Tikka

450g paneer (Indian cottage cheese), cut into 10cm cubes

1 green pepper (about 120g), cut into 10cm cubes

1 red onion (about 90g), cut into 10cm cubes

melted butter for basting

juice of ½ lemon or chaat masala powder

FOR THE GRAM (CHICKPEA) FLOUR PASTE

2 tbsp vegetable oil

2 heaped tbsp gram (chickpea) flour

FOR THE MARINADE

40g fresh coriander leaves

40g fresh mint leaves

2 garlic cloves

½ tsp garam masala

1 green bird's eye chilli

3 tbsp Greek yoghurt

salt to taste

TIP
. . . . . .
You can also cook the kebabs on a hot barbecue for 6–8 minutes, turning occasionally and basting with the melted butter.

Green marinades are used in most Indian preparations - in breads, meats, fish or even snacks. Here the coriander and mint marinade coats cubes of Indian cottage cheese to lend a lovely flavour. This is a super-quick dish to cook. The paneer cooks in a matter of minutes and soaks in the flavour of the marinade really well.

1. Preheat the oven to 200°C/400°F/Gas mark 6. Put 3–4 wooden skewers in water and leave them to soak.

2. Now make the gram flour paste. Place a frying pan over a low heat and add the oil. When hot, add the flour and stir continuously to make sure there are no lumps. Keeping the heat low, cook for 2 minutes or until the flour gives off a nutty aroma. Set aside to cool.

3. To make the marinade, put all the ingredients for it in a blender and blitz to a smooth paste, adding a couple of tablespoons of water if needed. Add the gram flour paste and stir well. Set aside in a bowl.

4. Add the paneer to the marinade, along with the pepper cubes and red onion. Mix well and marinate for up to an hour.

5. When ready to cook, thread the paneer and vegetables alternately onto the skewers. Place the skewers on a baking sheet in the preheated oven and cook for 8–10 minutes. The paneer should be soft, coated with the marinade and charred around the edges.

6. Sprinkle over the lemon juice or chaat masala and serve with Sticky Sweet Chilli Dipping Sauce (see page 221).

Bandhkopir Torkari...STIR-FRIED BENGALI FIVE-SPICE CABBAGE

2 tbsp vegetable oil

1 heaped tbsp panch puran (Bengali five-spice powder)

1 onion (about 100g), finely sliced

2.5cm piece of fresh root ginger, coarsely grated

½ tsp Kashmiri chilli powder or mild paprika

1 white cabbage (about 700g), finely shredded

salt to taste

FOR THE GARNISH

1 tbsp chopped fresh coriander

1 tsp lemon juice

Flavoured with the typical Bengali five-spice blend panch puran, this cabbage dish, using just a few ingredients, is probably one of the simplest ever!

1. Place a wok or deep sauté pan over a medium heat and add the oil. When hot, add the panch puran and fry for less than a minute to flavour the oil (see Tip). Add the onion and fry for 7–8 minutes or until it begins to soften.

2. Add the ginger and the chilli powder and cook for a minute. Tip in the cabbage and fry for 2 minutes, mixing well. Turn the heat to a low setting, cover and cook the cabbage for 6 minutes, stirring halfway through and making sure it doesn't stick to the bottom of the pan (you want the cabbage to cook all the way through but still retain a bite).

3. Season to taste, then garnish with the fresh coriander and lemon juice. Serve warm with a bread of your choice and some dal on the side.

TIP
. . . . . .
Make sure not to fry the panch puran spice mix for too long or it will become bitter and spoil the flavour of your dish. After frying, it should still be possible to detect the tangy and slightly sweet flavour of the fenugreek seeds that are part of it.

Jain-style Mattar Paneer

80g cashew nuts

1.5cm cassia bark

1 tsp cumin seeds

1 tsp fennel seeds

6 green cardamom
pods, seeds only

5 cloves

2 tomatoes (about
180g total weight),
blended to a pulp

1½ tbsp tomato purée

3 tbsp vegetable oil

¼ tsp garam masala

1 tsp Kashmiri chilli
powder or mild
paprika

½ tsp ground turmeric

1 tsp ground
coriander

100ml Greek yoghurt

350g paneer (Indian
cottage cheese), cut
into small cubes

100g frozen green
peas

salt to taste

FOR THE GARNISH

1 tbsp roughly
chopped fresh
coriander

1 tbsp lemon juice

Paneer (Indian cottage cheese) is a popular ingredient in Indian cooking and for obvious reasons: it not only has a beautiful texture, but also absorbs the flavours of spices superbly and takes just minutes to cook. Many Indian paneer dishes include spice pastes, and this Jain version has got to be my absolute favourite.

1. Soak the cashew nuts, cassia bark, all the seeds and cloves in some warm water for 20 minutes until slightly softened. Drain and place in a blender with 50ml water and blitz to a thick paste. Place in a bowl and set aside.

2. Add the tomatoes and tomato purée to the same blender, blitz to a thick paste and set aside.

3. Place a saucepan over a low heat and add the oil. When hot, add the cashew paste and fry for 2–3 minutes, stirring continuously to make sure it doesn't stick to the pan.

4. Add the tomato paste and sauté for a further 3 minutes or until the oil separates from the paste. Mix in the garam masala, chilli, turmeric and ground coriander and cook for 5 minutes on a low heat, stirring well until the colour starts to change.

5. Add the yoghurt, stirring continuously for 3–5 minutes to make sure it doesn't split, then add 150ml water. Season to taste and bring to a simmer. Cook over a low heat and add the paneer cubes along with the peas, stirring to coat in the sauce. Cook for 3–4 minutes or until the gravy is slightly thickened and the paneer is well coated.

6. Garnish with fresh coriander and lemon juice. Serve warm with naan or chapattis.

Achari Fish Tikka

1 tsp black/brown
mustard seeds

1½ tsp fennel seeds

1½ tsp cumin seeds

½ tsp nigella seeds

½ tsp fenugreek seeds

450g salmon fillets,
skinned and cut into
4cm chunks

100ml Greek yoghurt

3 garlic cloves

1 tsp hot green
chilli pickle

salt to taste

1 tbsp chopped fresh
coriander

1 tbsp melted butter
for basting

Here's a really quick recipe where the fish is marinated in a mixture of classic pickling spices and chilli and threaded onto skewers. I love making this for the family — stuffed in flatbread and served with chutney, it's such a fantastic dish when you're looking for an easy meal. And cutting the fish into chunks means it really doesn't take long to cook.

1. Put 3–4 wooden skewers in water and leave them to soak.

2. Coarsely crush all the seeds using a pestle and mortar (you still want a few whole, and crushing them lightly will just release their flavours). Place in a bowl, add the salmon and mix well.

3. Put 2 tablespoons of the yoghurt into a blender along with the garlic and green chilli pickle and blitz to a smooth paste. Add this and the remaining yoghurt to the salmon, then add the coriander and salt. Mix well and leave to marinate for 20 minutes.

4. Meanwhile, preheat the grill until medium hot. Put a wire rack over a baking tray and place the tray on the top shelf.

4. Thread the salmon onto the skewers and place them on the wire rack. Grill the fish tikkas for 10–12 minutes or until just done and slightly charred around the edges (the charring will add more flavour). Make sure to turn the skewers halfway through the cooking and baste with butter.

5. Serve the tikka with chapattis and Mint and Coriander Chutney (see page 225).

Bohra-style Fried Lamb Chops

12 garlic cloves

4cm piece of fresh root ginger

12–15 lamb chops, French-trimmed (ask your butcher to do this)

½ tsp ground turmeric

pinch of salt

90g plain flour for coating

2 eggs, beaten

90g fine white breadcrumbs

oil for frying

FOR THE MARINADE

2½ tsp Kashmiri chilli powder or mild paprika

1 heaped tsp ground cumin

2 tsp ground coriander

4 tbsp malt vinegar

salt to taste

This is a family recipe that was kindly given to me by a friend who hails from a Bohra Muslim household. The Bohra community is known for cooking some of the best meat dishes, including snacks, biryanis and dishes featuring goat meat. I ate these lamb chops at my friend's home quite a few times when I lived in India and always wondered how they were so perfect - spiced, succulent and with a delicious crumb coating. Here's the answer!

1. Blend the garlic to a paste in a wet paste grinder or a mini food processor. Reserve 1 tablespoon for the marinade and put the rest into a heavy-based saucepan. Blitz the ginger separately and add to the saucepan.

2. Add the lamb chops, turmeric, salt and 300ml water to the pan. Bring to a boil and simmer, covered, for 18–20 minutes on a low heat.

3. Meanwhile, make the masala marinade. Mix the ingredients for it in a bowl, along with 3 tablespoons of water. Add the reserved garlic paste and set aside.

4. Drain the chops and, while still warm, mix them with the marinade.

5. Place a frying pan over a medium heat and add 1cm of oil. Dip the chops in the flour, then the beaten egg, and finally the breadcrumbs. Fry them in batches for 2–3 minutes on each side until golden brown and crisp on the outside. Keep the cooked chops warm until the rest are fried.

6. Serve with Mint and Coriander Chutney (see page 225).

Maharashtrian Amti...LENTIL CURRY WITH TAMARIND AND COCONUT

250g toor dal (split pigeon peas)

1 tsp ground turmeric

2 tbsp vegetable oil

1 heaped tsp black/ brown mustard seeds

½ tsp cumin seeds

10 fresh curry leaves

pinch of asafoetida

1 green bird's eye chilli, slit lengthways

1 tbsp jaggery or sugar

2½ tsp tamarind paste (see Tip)

1 tsp Maharashtrian goda masala or garam masala

½ tsp Kashmiri chilli powder

salt to taste

FOR THE GARNISH

1 tbsp freshly grated coconut, or desiccated coconut soaked for 2 minutes in warm water and drained

chopped fresh coriander

This is the quintessential sweet and sour lentil curry and one that we devoured on numerous occasions when growing up in India. The use of jaggery and tamarind together may seem strange, but is quite common to dal made in the west of India. I love it with steaming hot rice, aamti poured over the top and a dollop of butter or ghee. Bliss!

1. Place a heavy-based saucepan over a high heat and add the dal, 1 litre of water and the turmeric. Bring to a boil and simmer gently for 45–50 minutes until the dal starts to get mushy. Stir well to make sure it doesn't stick to the bottom of the pan (add a splash of water if necessary). Turn off the heat and mash the dal slightly to thicken it. Cover and set aside.

2. Place another heavy-based saucepan over a medium heat, and add the oil. When hot, add the mustard seeds and fry for about a minute. As they begin to splutter, add the cumin seeds and curry leaves, working quickly. Fry for 20 seconds, then add the asafoetida and bird's eye chilli.

3. Tip in the cooked dal along with the jaggery, tamarind paste, goda masala, chilli powder and salt. Mix well and fry for a minute. Add 300ml water and simmer over a low heat for 3–5 minutes. Stir well.

4.Turn off the heat and garnish with the coconut and coriander. Serve warm with chapattis or rice.

TIP
......
Tamarind paste varies in strength, some brands being a lot stronger than others, so add it carefully and keep tasting your curry until you get the flavour you like.

Baingan ka Bharta...SMOKY AUBERGINE WITH SPICES, TOMATO AND GINGER

2–3 aubergines (about 500g total weight)

2 tbsp vegetable oil

2 green bird's eye chillies, slit lengthways

1 onion (about 110g)

4 garlic cloves, finely chopped

2 tomatoes (about 190g total weight), finely chopped

1 tsp tomato purée

½ ground turmeric

½ tsp mild chilli powder

salt to taste

FOR THE GARNISH

2 tbsp chopped fresh coriander

1 tbsp lemon juice

1.5cm piece of fresh root ginger, cut into julienne strips

TIP
......

In Step 1 you can, if you prefer, roast the aubergines in the oven at 200°C/400°F/ Gas mark 6 for 20–25 minutes. Make sure to prick them lightly with a fork before you put them in the oven so that the heat can penetrate them.

Using only aubergines and a few spices, this might seem like the simplest vegetarian dish, but what makes it so special is the way the aubergines are cooked. Charring them over an open flame means that a smoky, earthy flavour develops and lingers all the way through cooking this dish. With a natural warmth from the spices, this is home cooking at its best.

1. Hold the aubergines with tongs over an open flame set at a medium heat, turning every 5–7 minutes until they start to blacken all over and soften (this should take 15–18 minutes).

2. Place the aubergines over a plate and scrape off the skin — it should come off easily. Discard the skin and mash the aubergine flesh with the back of a fork. Set aside.

3. Place a heavy-based saucepan over a medium heat and add the oil. When hot, add the bird's eye chillies and fry for a few seconds. Add the onion and sauté on a medium heat for 8–10 minutes until it starts to change colour and soften.

4. Tip in the garlic and fry for 20–30 seconds, then add the tomatoes. Fry for about 5–6 minutes or until they have softened. Add the tomato purée along with the turmeric and chilli powder and cook for a minute.

5. Add the aubergines and mix well. Cook, covered, on a low heat for 2 minutes.

6. Season to taste and garnish with the fresh coriander, lemon juice and ginger. Mix and serve with dal and a bowl of rice.

Guntur-style Chicken Stir-fry

650g skinless, boneless chicken thighs

2 tbsp vegetable oil

1 tsp black/brown mustard seeds

8 fresh curry leaves

1 red onion (about 100g), thinly sliced

1 tbsp tomato purée

1 tsp ground coriander

1 tsp ground fennel

salt to taste

1 tbsp desiccated coconut

FOR THE PASTE
3 mild dried red chillies

1 tbsp cashew nuts, roughly chopped

80ml warm water

2.5cm piece of fresh root ginger, roughly chopped

4 cloves

1 tsp ground black pepper

FOR THE GARNISH
1.5cm piece of fresh root ginger, cut into slivers

1 tbsp chopped fresh coriander

Hailing from the Guntur region of India in Andhra, this rustic dish uses traditional spices, including black pepper and fennel. Leftover roast chicken can be used instead of fresh if you wish.

1. First make the paste. Soak the chillies and cashew nuts in the warm water for 20 minutes to soften. Transfer them to a blender, along with 30ml of their soaking liquid. Add the rest of the paste ingredients and blitz until smooth.

2. Boil 500ml water in a small saucepan, add the chicken thighs and let them simmer over a low heat for 7–8 minutes until they're succulent and cooked through. Reserve 100–120ml of the stock and set aside. When the chicken is cool enough to handle, roughly shred it onto a plate.

3. Place a heavy-based saucepan over a medium heat and add the oil. When hot, add the mustard seeds and curry leaves. Let them splutter for a few seconds, then add the sliced onion and fry for 6–7 minutes until it starts to soften.

4. Turn the heat down to a low setting and add the chilli paste and tomato purée; fry for 2 minutes, stirring continuously to make sure the mixture doesn't stick to the bottom of the pan (add a splash of water if necessary).

5. Add the ground coriander and fennel along with some salt. Fry for a few seconds, then add 100ml of the reserved chicken stock (plus a little more if too dry) and simmer over a low heat for 1 minute. Add the shredded chicken and stir well to coat the pieces thoroughly. Add the coconut, cover and simmer for a further 3 minutes until everything is well mixed and the coconut dissolves.

6. Remove from the heat and garnish with the ginger and fresh coriander.

Bengali Begun Bhaja...QUICK-FRIED
AUBERGINES WITH TURMERIC AND CHILLI

2 aubergines (about
900g total weight)
1 tsp ground turmeric
1 tsp Kashmiri chilli
powder or mild paprika
mustard or vegetable
oil for frying
salt to taste

Ask a Bengali what defines comfort food and
the chances are that Begun Bhaja will be
top of that list, alongside some dal and
plain rice. The quintessential elements of
eating for most Indians would always include
a staple like dal and rice with something
fried on the side for that added spiced,
crispy texture. This recipe is really simple
and uses just a few basic spices. Make sure
you do the proper Bengali or Bong ritual and
serve it with a warm bowl of lentil curry and
rice. It'll keep you coming back for seconds.

1. Slice the aubergines into 2cm discs. Mix the
spices with the salt and rub into the aubergine
slices.

2. Place a frying pan over a medium heat and add
some oil. Add the aubergine slices in batches and
fry for 2-3 minutes on each side until golden
brown. Drain on kitchen paper and repeat with the
remaining slices, adding more oil if necessary.

3. Serve as a snack either on their own, or
accompanied by dal and rice.

Amritsari Macchi...FRIED FISH WITH CAROM SEEDS, CHILLI AND GINGER

300g skinless boneless white fish fillets (cod or haddock would be great), cut into bite-sized pieces

½ tsp ground turmeric

3 tbsp malt vinegar

4cm piece of fresh root ginger, roughly chopped

2 garlic cloves, roughly chopped

30g gram (chickpea) flour

½ tsp ajwain (carom) seeds

1 tsp Kashmiri chilli powder or mild paprika

½ tsp baking powder

1 tsp chopped fresh coriander

1 heaped tbsp Greek yoghurt

oil for deep-frying

salt to taste

chaat masala or lemon juice to garnish

A classic Punjabi fried fish coated in a gram flour batter that includes spices and coriander. Crispy and delicious — like an Indian fish buttie snack!

1. Put the fish pieces in a bowl and sprinkle with the turmeric and 1 tablespoon of the vinegar. Mix well and leave to marinate.

2. Pound the ginger and garlic to a paste using a pestle and mortar.

3. Put the gram flour, ajwain seeds, chilli powder, baking powder, coriander and salt into a bowl. Add the ginger, garlic, yoghurt and remaining vinegar. Mix really well to a thick paste, making sure there are no lumps. Now rub the paste over the fish pieces and leave to marinate for 10—15 minutes.

4. Heat a deep-fat fryer to 170°C or fill a large saucepan or kadhai (deep wok) one-third full of oil and heat until a cube of bread dropped into the hot oil sizzles and turns golden brown in 30 seconds. Add the fish pieces to the hot oil in batches and deep-fry until crisp around the edges and golden brown.

5. Garnish with chaat masala or lemon juice and serve warm stuffed into bread rolls.

Murghi na Farcha...PARSI-STYLE CHICKEN WITH NUTMEG AND CUMIN

1 heaped tsp cumin seeds

½ tsp ground cinnamon

pinch of ground cloves

3 garlic cloves

4cm piece of fresh root ginger

2 green bird's eye chillies

1 tbsp malt vinegar

1 tbsp Worcestershire sauce

2 tbsp plain flour

8 skinless chicken drumsticks

oil for deep-frying

2 eggs, beaten

salt to taste

A Parsi speciality, this deep-fried chicken recipe takes it up a notch. Served at weddings and celebrations, it's very more-ish, with a hint of the spices that are synonymous with the Parsi community, including nutmeg and Worcestershire sauce. Yes, believe it or not, the latter is the secret ingredient in many Indian dishes.

1.Preheat the oven to 200°C/400°F/Gas mark 6.

2. Coarsely grind the cumin seeds using a pestle and mortar. Tip into a mixing bowl and add the ground cinnamon and cloves.

3. Put the garlic, ginger and bird's eye chillies into a food processor or blender and blitz to a coarse paste. Put the paste in the same bowl as the ground spices, then add the vinegar and Worcestershire sauce. Mix well and add the flour, salt and 20ml water to form a thick paste.

4. Score the drumsticks and mix with the marinade, making sure to push the marinade into the slits in the chicken flesh. Set aside for a couple of hours or preferably overnight.

5. When ready to cook, heat a deep-fat fryer to 170°C or fill a large saucepan or kadhai (deep wok) one-third full of oil and heat until a cube of bread dropped into the hot oil sizzles and turns golden brown in 30 seconds.

6. Dip the chicken drumsticks in the beaten egg and deep-fry them in batches for 3–4 minutes until golden brown. Drain on kitchen paper.

7. Put the pieces in a baking tray and place in the preheated oven for 20 minutes, until cooked through.

8. Serve with a raita and/or chutney of your choice.

Gajar ki Barfi...SLOW-COOKED CARROT FUDGE WITH CARDAMOM AND PISTACHIO

750g carrots, grated
150ml double cream
200ml condensed milk
1 tsp freshly ground cardamom seeds
2 tbsp raisins
handful of mixed almonds and pistachios, roughly chopped
180g full-fat milk powder

Here's the ever-popular north Indian carrot pudding, but this time made into a deliciously moist fudge. Eaten in the winter months when carrots are at their best, nothing beats these sweet little squares, which are infused with cardamom and full of nuts and raisins.

1. Line a 23 x 23cm baking dish with greaseproof paper and set aside.

2. Place a saucepan over a medium heat. Add the carrots, cream and condensed milk and cook for 35–40 minutes, stirring frequently, until the mixture thickens slightly and the carrots have absorbed most of the liquid.

3. Add the ground cardamom, raisins and a few of the nuts. Now, working quickly, add the milk powder a few tablespoons at a time. Stir for about 5 minutes until the powder is mixed in and there are no lumps.

4. Tip the mixture into the lined baking dish and smooth out the edges with the back of a spoon. Sprinkle over the remaining chopped nuts. Cool and then refrigerate for a few hours, or preferably overnight.

5. Cut into bite-sized squares and serve with a nice cup of tea.

Maharashtrian Sheera...SEMOLINA COOKED
IN BUTTER, CARDAMOM AND SAFFRON

6 green cardamom
pods, seeds only
70g sugar
pinch of saffron
50g softened butter
100g coarse semolina

FOR THE GARNISH
1 tbsp butter
handful of cashew
nuts, broken
handful of raisins

If there's anything that tastes delicious with copious amounts of butter, this dessert is most definitely it! Mum always used to make it for us when we were growing up, so as well as being a traditional part of the Maharashtrian community, it's also something that always reminds me of home. One of the reasons I really enjoy making this dish is because of its wonderful combination of flavours. Creamy semolina with saffron, ground cardamom and, of course, all that yummy butter. Even the cashew nuts and raisins are fried in it. It's got to be good!

1. Crush the cardamom seeds to a powder using a pestle and mortar.

2. Put the sugar, saffron and 150ml water into a small saucepan. Bring to a simmer and continue simmering until the sugar has dissolved. Set aside.

3. Meanwhile, add 40g of the butter to a separate saucepan and gently melt on a low heat. Add the semolina and roast, stirring continuously, for 7–8 minutes until it starts to go light brown and gives out a nutty roasted aroma (make sure to keep stirring as it can burn very quickly). Add the ground cardamom and the remaining butter.

4. Now add the saffron-infused water a little at a time over a low heat, stirring continuously as the mixture starts to come together. Cover, remove from the heat and set aside.

5. To make the garnish, melt the butter in a frying pan and fry the cashew nuts and raisins for a minute until they change colour and go light brown. Add to the Sheera, mix well and serve warm or at room temperature.

Shrikhand...YOGHURT, SAFFRON AND CARDAMOM PUDDING

1kg Greek yoghurt

generous pinch of saffron

125g caster sugar

¼ tsp freshly ground cardamom

roughly chopped pistachios and pomegranate seeds to garnish

A traditional authentic dessert made by my community in Mumbai, and one that I will always remember as being a family effort. Mum would fry the puris while Dad helped to make the yoghurt mix with sugar. And, of course, I helped eat it all!

1. Put the yoghurt in a piece of muslin, tie the corners together and leave over a sieve to drain for 2 hours.

2. Soak the saffron in a couple of tablespoons of warm water for about 15 minutes.

3. When ready, put the yoghurt into a large bowl, add the sugar and mix well. Now add the ground cardamom, the saffron strands and their water and leave to chill in the refrigerator for a few hours

4. Serve in dessert bowls garnished with pistachios and pomegranate seeds for a lovely colour or topped with fresh fruit of your choice. I prefer eating this with puris but of course it can always be served at the end of the meal for dessert.

TIPS
......
As Greek yoghurt is already thick, I don't always bother to strain it if I'm in a rush (a cardinal sin by my mother's standards). I must admit, though, that straining does give a richer, creamier consistency. However, it is important to soak the saffron in order to get the maximum colour and flavour from it.

Photograph overleaf

INDULGENT

अनुग्रहशील

Indulge *verb*
to allow someone to have anything they want; to pamper or spoil them.
to give into (a desire, taste, wish, etc) without restraint.
to eat or drink, usually freely or without restraint.

My style of cooking has always been about hearty meals, aromatic spices and traditional Indian dishes to awaken the senses. I am most happy when putting lots of love into a warm pot of curry such as the KERALAN KOZHI KUTTAN (page 140) simmering on my hob or preparing my favourite MUMBAI FRANKIE ROLLS (page 122) which I remember eating on the streets of Dadar in Mumbai, aged 6. Mum would buy them as a quick fix for a meal but one was never enough and my recipe is reminiscent of that, with succulent meat chunks coated in spices, topped with chutney, pickled onions and chillies rolled in layered parathas and is just as moreish. I don't know any other rolls or wraps that come close to this one in terms of flavour, texture and taste. So you know what you need to try now!

The recipes in this chapter might take a little bit longer to make but once devoured you will know exactly why it was so very worth the effort. Take the time to really enjoy the sensations and dive in the world of spices. The grinding, marinating and frying means the divine scents of CHUKHANDAR KA GOSHT (beetroot and lamb curry, page 144) will be wafting through the house. Or enjoy biting into a deep-fried, sandwiched BREAD PAKODA (page 120) — crisp, coated with batter and stuffed with a spiced potato mix! One of my very favourite recipes, MURGH KALI MIRCH (black pepper chicken, page 134) needs time to marinate but otherwise needs only a little attention before you have a treat for the taste buds.

Whether cooking a special meal for your partner or rustling up a leisurely meal for family and friends, this chapter is for when you are relaxed and ready to savour something truly delicious.

All recipes serve 4.

Dabeli...SPICED GUJARATI POTATO SANDWICH WITH TAMARIND AND COCONUT

2 tbsp vegetable oil

1 onion (about 50g), finely chopped

4 potatoes (about 550g), boiled then coarsely grated into a bowl

pinch of sugar

juice of ½ lemon

3 tbsp desiccated coconut

3 tbsp finely chopped fresh coriander

40g fresh pomegranate seeds

45g roasted peanuts, roughly chopped

salt to taste

FOR THE DABELI MASALA

¼ tsp ground cinnamon

½ tsp ground cumin

1 tsp Kashmiri chilli powder or mild paprika

1 tsp ground coriander

TO ASSEMBLE

8 soft white rolls

4 tsp softened butter

Sticky Sweet Chilli Dipping Sauce (see page 221)

Tamarind Chutney (see page 222)

1 red onion (about 50g), finely chopped

sev (crunchy chickpea strands)

Anyone who's been to Mumbai or even cities in the west of India must have eaten this little beauty, but it still amazes me how little people in the UK know about it. Nothing would make me happier than seeing a street stall serving Dabeli in London. Well, maybe after this recipe they just might! This delicious potato cake is made with herbs, ground spices, peanuts and pomegranate, then stuffed in pan-fried white buns with a squeeze of lemon and accompanied by lashings of chutneys. Sounds good? It is!

1. First make the dabeli masala. Mix all the ingredients for it in a bowl and set aside.

2. To make the potato cake, place a small frying pan over a low heat and add the oil. When hot, add the onion and fry for 3—4 minutes. Add the dabeli masala and stir for a few seconds, then follow with the grated potato, stirring well for about 2 minutes to make sure it's mixed in. Add the sugar, lemon juice, desiccated coconut, coriander, pomegranate, peanuts and salt. Turn off the heat and transfer the potato cake to a warmed plate.

3. To assemble the dabeli, cut open 2 adjacent sides of the bread rolls: this leaves each roll still joined on 2 sides and creates a pocket of sorts. Heat the butter in the emptied potato cake pan and fry the top and bottom of the rolls over a medium heat for 1—2 minutes each side until they crisp up. (You might have to do this in batches, allowing ½ teaspoon butter per roll.)

4. Now fill the rolls. Spread a layer of the chilli chutney inside the roll, along with a little Tamarind Chutney. Add 2 heaped tablespoons of the potato dabeli mix, followed by a handful of red onions, a sprinkling of sev and a bit more of the Tamarind Chutney. Eat!

Bread Pakoda...DEEP-FRIED POTATO SANDWICHES

MAKES 8 SANDWICH TRIANGLES

4 slices of white bread
oil for deep-frying

FOR THE POTATO MIX

2 tbsp vegetable oil
pinch of asafoetida
1 tsp black/brown mustard seeds
7–10 fresh curry leaves
1 green bird's eye chilli, finely chopped
4cm piece of fresh root ginger, finely chopped
½ tsp ground turmeric
4–5 potatoes (600g total weight), boiled then roughly crushed (see Tip)
60g frozen green peas
salt to taste

FOR THE BATTER

150g gram (chickpea) flour
½ tsp ground turmeric
½ tsp Kashmiri chilli powder or mild paprika
salt to taste

This street food snack is made all across the city of Mumbai and beyond. Food stalls make it in minutes and, like most street food, it's cheap as chips. It used to be my 'go to' guilty pleasure and one that I still indulge in. What always gets me is the spicy potato mix encased in a crispy coating of gram flour. Every bite, washed down with a warm cup of tea, was (and still is!) pure pleasure. Watching street hawkers deep-frying the pakoda while I waited in anticipation of taking the first bite was always what made scoffing it down that much more satisfying.

1. First make the potato mix. Place a heavy-based pan over a medium heat and add the oil. When hot, add the asafoetida followed by the mustard seeds and fry until they begin to splutter.

2. Add the curry leaves and bird's eye chilli. Fry for a minute, then add the ginger and fry for a few seconds. Tip in the turmeric, give it a quick stir and let the spices cook for a further 30 seconds. Add the potatoes and green peas, stirring well to make sure the mixture is evenly coloured and flavoured. Cover and steam on a low heat for 2 minutes. Stir again, garnish with the coriander, add the lemon juice and season to taste. Leave to cool slightly while you make the batter.

3. Put the gram flour into a mixing bowl and add the turmeric, chilli powder and salt. Add a little water and whisk to make a smooth batter (you're looking for a double cream sort of consistency).

4. Place a slice of bread on a plate and spread with the spiced potato mix. Place another slice over the first to make a sandwich, pressing lightly to make sure the filling is compact, then cut the sandwich diagonally. Repeat with the rest of the bread and potato mix.

Continued opposite

FOR THE GARNISH
1 tbsp roughly
chopped fresh
coriander
juice of ½ lemon

5. Heat a deep-fat fryer to 170°C or fill a large saucepan or kadhai (deep wok) one-third full of oil and heat until a cube of bread dropped into the hot oil sizzles and turns golden brown in 30 seconds. Dip each potato sandwich in the gram flour batter and deep-fry until light brown and crisp all over. Drain on kitchen paper.

6. Cut the bread pakoda into smaller pieces and serve warm with a chutney of your choice. I love it with Red Chilli Coconut Chutney (see page 224)

TIP
· · · · · ·

The potato mix is easy to make, but is best crushed by hand as you want a slightly lumpy mix rather than a smooth mashed potato base. Once mixed with the spices, it can be eaten as it is (without frying), either on its own or stuffed in chapattis or bread.

Mumbai Frankie Rolls

MAKES 4 ROLLS

4cm piece of fresh
root ginger

4 garlic cloves

1 tbsp malt vinegar

½ tsp Kashmiri chilli
powder or mild
paprika

¼ tsp garam masala

½ tsp ground cumin

1 tsp Greek yoghurt

400g boned leg of
lamb, diced into
bite-sized pieces

2 tbsp vegetable oil

salt to taste

TO ASSEMBLE

2 green bird's eye
chillies, finely
chopped

30ml malt vinegar

1 red onion (about
100g), thinly sliced

juice of ½ lemon

4 frozen parathas

2 eggs, lightly
beaten

Mint and Coriander
Chutney (see page
225)

TIP
......

Ready-frozen parathas
made with maida flour
(a mixture of hard
and soft wheat) work
best with the egg, but
chapattis or plain
flatbread could be used
instead.

Frankies are rolls made with flatbread and egg stuffed with spicy fried meat chunks, salad onions and some mint chutney. The first bite of a Frankie will keep you hooked forever.

1. Pound the ginger and garlic to a coarse paste using a pestle and mortar. Put the paste in a large bowl and add the vinegar, chilli powder, garam masala and cumin. Stir well, then add the yoghurt. Add the lamb and mix well to coat the meat thoroughly. Leave to marinate for a few hours or preferably overnight.

2. When ready to cook, start to prepare the assembly ingredients. Put the chopped chillies in a small bowl, add the vinegar and set aside to soak. In a separate bowl mix the red onion with the lemon juice and a generous pinch of salt. Mix well and let them soak too while you fry the lamb.

3. Place a frying pan over a medium heat and add the oil. When hot, add the lamb and fry for 12–15 minutes, stirring continually to make sure it doesn't dry out or stick to the pan (add a splash of water – around 20ml – if necessary). Season to taste and remove from the heat. Keep warm while you assemble the frankies.

4. Heat a separate dry frying pan and add a paratha to cook it through for 2–3 minutes. Flip it over and add 3 tablespoons of the beaten egg, spreading it well over the paratha. Let the underside cook, then flip it again to cook the eggs for a few seconds. The paratha will begin to fluff up and form a pillowy base for the stuffing.

5. Transfer the paratha to a plate. Place a small portion of the cooked spicy lamb on it, add a few onion slices and spread over 2 teaspoons of chutney. Sprinkle 1 teaspoon of the chilli-flavoured vinegar over the top. Roll up the Frankie and wrap in foil or secure with a toothpick. Repeat with the other parathas and eat while still warm.

Haraa Bharaa Tikkis...SPINACH, PEA
AND POTATO CAKES

**MAKES 10-12
TIKKIS**

1 tsp cumin seeds

180g spinach

2-3 potatoes (about
400g), boiled and
coarsely grated

80g frozen green
peas, defrosted

2.5cm piece of fresh
root ginger

2 green bird's eye
chillies

handful of finely
chopped fresh
coriander

1 heaped tsp cornflour

1 tsp lemon juice

oil for frying

salt

Although these spicy potato cakes can be eaten just as they are, in India they are often shaped around skewers and eaten as vegetarian kebabs. Made with spinach, peas, coriander and chillies, and greatly enjoyed with chilli or tamarind chutney, tikkis are hugely popular snacks amongst Indians.

1. Lightly dry-roast the cumin seeds in a frying pan for 1 minute, shaking the pan every so often to make sure they don't burn. Cool slightly, then grind coarsely using a pestle and mortar.

2. Plunge the spinach in hot water for a few seconds, squeeze out as much water as possible and chop finely. Add to a bowl along with the potatoes, green peas and ground cumin.

3. Crush the ginger and bird's eye chillies to a coarse paste using a pestle and mortar and add to the vegetable mixture. Add the coriander, cornflour, lemon juice and salt. Mix well and cover with cling film. Refrigerate for 15 minutes.

4. When ready, divide the mixture into 10—12 equal portions around 6cm wide. Place a frying pan over a medium heat and add the oil. When hot, fry the tikkis in batches for 2—3 minutes on each side until crisp around the edges and light brown. Drain on kitchen paper and serve warm with Sticky Sweet Chilli Dipping Sauce or Tamarind Chutney (see page 221 or 222).

Chingri Malai Curry...BENGALI-STYLE
PRAWN CURRY

12–15 large raw prawns, shelled and deveined, tails left on

½ tsp ground turmeric

4 tbsp vegetable oil

4 green cardamom pods

3 cloves

2 bay leaves

¼ tsp Kashmiri chilli powder or mild paprika

½ tsp sugar

100ml coconut milk

¼ tsp English mustard

salt to taste

roughly chopped fresh coriander to garnish

FOR THE ONION PASTE

1 onion (about 50g), roughly chopped

2.5cm piece of fresh root ginger, roughly chopped

2 garlic cloves, roughly chopped

2 green bird's eye chillies

50g freshly grated coconut, or 80g desiccated coconut soaked for 2 minutes in warm water and drained

One of our family favourites and a recipe I was given by our Bengali neighbour when I lived in India. Cooking the curry in mustard, chilli and coconut milk is a winning combination, and adding the prawns at the end of cooking ensures they are sweet and succulent. I would normally fry the prawns in mustard oil before adding them to the curry because it has a pungent flavour that's perfect with the sweetness of the prawns, but here I have altered the original recipe slightly to include English mustard in the curry itself, which gives similar results.

1. Put the prawns in a bowl. Mix in the turmeric and a pinch of salt, then set aside.

2. Put all the ingredients for the onion paste in a blender. Add a splash of water and blitz to a smooth thick paste. Set aside.

3. Place a frying pan over a medium heat and add 2 tablespoons of the oil. When hot, add the prawns and fry for 20 seconds on each side until they start to colour (don't cook them all the way through). Drain on kitchen paper and set aside.

4. Heat the remaining oil in a heavy-based saucepan. Add the cardamom pods, cloves and bay leaves; fry for 30 seconds. Now tip in the onion paste and fry over a medium heat for 5–7 minutes, stirring frequently to make sure it doesn't stick to the bottom of the pan. Add the chilli powder, sugar and salt. Stir for a further minute then add the coconut milk and 100ml water. Bring to a boil and simmer on a low heat. Add the prawns and simmer for 3–4 minutes until they are cooked all the way through.

5. Put the mustard in a bowl and thin out with a tablespoon of water. Mix well and add to the curry. Garnish with fresh coriander and serve warm with boiled rice.

Bharli Wangi...STUFFED BABY AUBERGINES WITH COCONUT AND TAMARIND

8–10 baby aubergines, slit lengthways, but kept together at the stems

3 tbsp vegetable oil

2 green bird's eye chillies, slit lengthways

salt to taste

FOR THE PASTE

2 heaped tsp coriander seeds

½ tsp Kashmiri chilli powder or mild paprika

50g cashew nuts or roasted peanuts

20g fresh coriander stems

2 tbsp desiccated coconut, soaked for 2 minutes in warm water and drained

4–5 garlic cloves

1 tbsp ground jaggery or brown sugar

1½ tsp tamarind paste

FOR THE GARNISH

2 tsp desiccated coconut

1 tbsp chopped fresh coriander

When used in Indian cuisine, aubergines (or 'brinjal', as they are known) are cooked through, offering depth to the curry and a rich flavour. The purple colour deepens and absorbs all the flavours from the curry almost like a sponge. This Marathi recipe, in which fried aubergines are stuffed with a spicy filling made with peanut, cane sugar, powdered spices and lime, is a family favourite.

1. First make the paste. Mix together all the ingredients for it in a bowl, add 30–40ml water and mix well. Transfer to a food processor and blitz to a thick paste. Stuff some of the paste into the aubergine slits and set the rest aside.

2. Place a deep heavy-based pan over a medium heat and add the oil. When hot, add the bird's eye chillies and let them sizzle for a few seconds to infuse the oil. Add the aubergines and fry them in the oil for a minute, turning them over as they seal and change colour. Drain on kitchen paper and set aside.

3. Turn the heat to low, scrape up any leftover paste from the stuffing, add the reserved paste, and stir-fry for 1–2 minutes. Add 300ml water and season to taste. Bring the curry to a boil, then simmer on a low heat. Add the aubergines and stir gently, making sure they are coated in the gravy. Cook, covered, on a low heat for 15–17 minutes until the aubergines are tender and the curry thickens slightly. (Make sure you stir the curry a few times during cooking so that it doesn't stick to the bottom of the pan.)

4. Garnish with desiccated coconut and chopped coriander and serve with chapattis and raita.

Photograph on previous page

Aloo ke Parathe...FLATBREAD STUFFED WITH SPICED POTATO

MAKES 6 PARATHAS

300g wholewheat or chapatti flour, plus extra for dusting

pinch of salt

3 tbsp vegetable oil

butter for frying

FOR THE FILLING

2–3 potatoes (about 360g), boiled and crushed

1 tsp coarsely ground cumin seeds

5cm piece of fresh root ginger, grated

1 green bird's eye chilli, finely chopped

2½ tsp amchoor (dry mango powder)

¼ tsp Kashmiri chilli powder or mild paprika

3 tbsp finely chopped fresh coriander

salt to taste

This traditional Punjabi flatbread stuffed with spiced potatoes, chillies, ginger and ground spices is pan-fried in buttery goodness and is one of my all-time favourites, especially as all it needs is some yoghurt or pickle as an accompaniment. My husband loves them too, and one of the first things I was asked by my mother-in-law when we met for the first time was if I knew how to cook them. I said yes, even though I didn't, but quickly made sure I perfected them.

1. Sift the flour and salt together in a bowl. Add the oil and enough water (about 220ml) to form a soft dough. Knead well for 5–7 minutes until smooth. Wrap in cling film or cover with a damp cloth and set aside to rest.

2. Meanwhile, put all the filling ingredients into a large bowl and mix well.

3. Now divide the dough into 6 equal portions and roll each into a ball. One at a time, flatten the dough balls and roll out on a lightly floured surface to a disc 7cm in diameter. Cup a disc in the palm of your hand and put some potato filling (about 2 tbsp) into the hollow. Pull the edges together to enclose the filling completely. Seal well and flatten.

4. Dust the stuffed dough with flour and roll out again into a 15cm diameter circle (don't roll it out too thinly or the dough will split, but if it does split slightly, it's fine to reseal and fry).

5. Put a flat griddle or heavy-based frying pan over a low heat and add 1 teaspoon of butter to the pan. When it's hot, shake the excess flour off the paratha and place it in the hot pan. Cook on a low heat for 4–5 minutes, then smear a little melted butter over the surface with the back of a spoon. Now flip it over and fry the other side for the same time, until the paratha is cooked and has brown speckles. Wrap in foil to keep warm while you cook the rest.

6. Serve with yoghurt and your choice of pickle.

Bengali Prawn Cakes

MAKES 8–10 CAKES

250g raw tiger prawns, shelled and deveined

200g skinless boneless cod

½ tsp ground turmeric

1 tsp chilli flakes

½ tsp garam masala

10 fresh curry leaves, roughly chopped

2 tbsp finely chopped fresh coriander

2 tsp English mustard

1 tsp gram (chickpea) flour

oil for shallow-frying

squeeze of lemon juice or chaat masala

salt to taste

This recipe is adapted from a traditional Bengali paturi, where fishcakes or prawn cakes are wrapped and cooked in banana leaves, which impart a really lovely flavour. I made this with sweet prawns, which work brilliantly with the chilli and turmeric. For me it wouldn't be complete without mustard, and English mustard works so well alongside the prawns.

1. Put half the prawns and half the cod into a food processor and, pulsing frequently, blitz to a coarse paste. Transfer to a bowl. Finely chop the rest of the prawns and cod into little chunks and add to the bowl.

2. Add the turmeric, chilli and garam masala along with the curry leaves, coriander, mustard, gram flour and salt and stir well (the mixture will be a little sticky, which is how it should be to help it bind together). Divide into 8–10 equal portions and shape into round cakes.

3. Place a frying pan over a medium heat and add the oil. When hot, add the prawn cakes a few at a time, frying for 2–3 minutes on each side until they are crisp and light brown.

4. Serve with a squeeze of lemon juice or some chaat masala and Sticky Sweet Chilli Dipping Sauce (see page 221).

Photograph on previous page

Achari Murgh...CHICKEN WITH TOMATO AND PICKLING SPICES

3 tbsp mustard oil or vegetable oil

4 dried red chillies

1 tsp fenugreek seeds

1 tsp black/brown mustard seeds

1 tsp cumin seeds

1 tsp fennel seeds

1 tsp nigella (onion) seeds

1 onion (about 170g), finely sliced

2 tbsp ginger and garlic paste (made with 8 garlic cloves and 5cm of ginger)

½ tsp ground turmeric

1½ tsp Kashmiri chilli powder or mild paprika

1½ tbsp tomato purée

800g chicken on the bone, skinned and cut into medium-sized pieces (ask your butcher to do this)

100ml natural yoghurt, lightly beaten

1 tsp lemon juice

salt to taste

chopped fresh coriander to garnish

A typical Rajasthani dish with 'pickling spices' — a mixture of whole spices, including nigella seeds, fennel and cumin — cooked with moist pieces of chicken on the bone for maximum flavour. A tomato and yoghurt base helps thicken the rich gravy. If you can find mustard oil, it does add that extra edge to this dish.

1. Place a heavy-based saucepan over a medium heat and add the mustard oil. When hot, add the dried chillies followed by all the seeds. Fry for about 20 seconds until they start to sizzle and pop.

2. Add the sliced onion and fry for 7–8 minutes until softened and light brown in colour. Add the ginger and garlic paste and stir for a further minute. Mix in the turmeric and chilli powder and fry over a medium heat for 20–30 seconds, stirring to make sure the mixture doesn't stick to the bottom off the pan (add a splash of water if necessary). Add the tomato purée and cook for a couple of minutes.

3. Add the chicken and cook for 5–7 minutes, making sure the pieces are sealed and coated in the spices. Add 100ml water and bring the curry to a boil, then simmer, covered, over a low heat for 25 minutes until the chicken is cooked through and succulent, stirring a couple of times while cooking. Add the yoghurt and stir, making sure not to let it heat for too long — just 5–7 minutes is enough.

4. Add the lemon juice and salt to taste, then garnish with the coriander. Serve hot with naan or Indian flatbread. Enjoy!

Murgh Kali Mirch...BLACK PEPPER CHICKEN

2.5cm piece of fresh
root ginger
8 garlic cloves
½ tsp coarsely ground
black peppercorns
1 tsp coarsely ground
white peppercorns
800g chicken on the
bone, skinned and
jointed (ask your
butcher to do this)
3 tbsp vegetable oil
2 green bird's eye
chillies, slit
lengthways
2 onions (about 190g
total weight), thinly
sliced
1 heaped tsp ground
coriander
salt to taste

FOR THE GARNISH
1 tsp lemon juice
1 tbsp chopped fresh
coriander to garnish

Long before chilli was ever part of Indian food, black pepper was the preferred spice for adding heat to curries. Murgh Kali Mirch is a dry-fry dish where chicken is fried with coarsely ground black pepper, lots of garlic and green bird's eye chillies, and, while not having a lot of sauce, manages to be utterly moist and succulent.

1. Put the ginger and garlic in a blender or food processor, add a splash of water and blitz to a fine paste. Put the paste into a mixing bowl with the crushed peppercorns. Add the chicken, stir well and and marinate for 2—3 hours or preferably overnight.

2. When ready to cook the chicken, place a wok or kadhai over a low heat and add the oil. When hot, add the bird's eye chillies and fry for a few seconds. Add the onions and fry for 8—10 minutes until they begin to soften and change colour.

3. Add the marinated chicken and fry over a medium heat to seal for 10 minutes. Sprinkle over the ground coriander and fry for a further 5 minutes, making sure the chicken pieces are fully coated with the spices. Season to taste.

4. Add 2 tablespoons of water to create a bit of steam, cover and simmer over a low heat for 20 minutes, stirring halfway through cooking, until the chicken is thoroughly cooked.

5. Remove the lid and cook for a further 8 minutes. Add the lemon juice and fresh coriander to garnish and serve warm with parathas and Tadka Dal (see page 50).

Lamb Dalcha...LAMB AND LENTIL STEW

3 tbsp vegetable oil

5 green cardamom pods

1 black cardamom pod

5cm cassia bark

6 cloves

1 bay leaf

2 small onions (about 110g total weight), thinly sliced

4 garlic cloves, finely chopped

2.5cm piece of fresh root ginger, finely chopped

1 tsp ground turmeric

1 tsp ground coriander

800g shoulder of lamb on the bone, chopped into bite-sized pieces (ask your butcher to do this)

2 tomatoes (about 180g total weight), roughly chopped

FOR THE DAL

200g masoor dal (red lentils)

pinch of ground turmeric

salt to taste

A traditional curry in which lamb chunks are cooked with coriander and spices and simmered with lentils. My fondest memories are of Mum cooking this for us on a Sunday afternoon along with rice and some raita. Sitting around a table with this delicious pot of stew at its centre felt like very special family time.

1. First make the dal. Rinse the lentils and put them in a medium pan with 900ml water, the turmeric and a pinch of salt. Bring to a boil and simmer for 25–30 minutes until cooked. Mash the dal with a potato masher so it thickens slightly.

2. To make the herb paste, put all the ingredients for it into a blender with 70ml water and blitz to a smooth thick paste. Set aside.

3. Now make the stew. Place a heavy-based wide pan over a medium heat and add the oil. When hot add all the cardamom pods, the cassia bark, cloves and bay leaf. Fry for 10–15 seconds so that the spices infuse the oil, then add the onions and sauté for 10–12 minutes or until they have softened and changed colour. Add the garlic and ginger and fry for 30 seconds. Now add the green herb paste and fry for 2 minutes, stirring well.

4. Add the turmeric and coriander, stirring well, and fry for 20 seconds. Now add the lamb and fry for 6–7 minutes, coating the meat with all the spices. Add the tomatoes and fry for a further minute, then add 100ml water and season to taste.

5. Bring the stew to a boil and simmer, covered, for 50 minutes, stirring halfway through cooking.

Continued opposite

FOR THE HERB PASTE

20g fresh mint leaves

60g fresh coriander leaves and stems

2 garlic cloves

FOR THE TADKA

1 tbsp vegetable oil

1 tsp cumin seeds

1 dried mild chilli

12 fresh curry leaves

FOR THE GARNISH

chopped fresh coriander

1 tbsp lemon juice

6. Add the mashed lentils to the stew and cook for a further 15 minutes, uncovered, over a low heat, stirring continuously to make sure the mixture doesn't stick to the bottom of the pan.

7. Just before serving, make the tadka. Place a small saucepan over a medium heat and add the oil. When hot, add the cumin seeds. Let them sizzle for 20—30 seconds, then add the dried chilli and curry leaves. Remove from the heat and stir the tadka into the stew.

8. Garnish the finished dish with coriander and lemon juice. Serve warm with chapattis or pulao rice and some raita.

TIP
......
The type of lentil used for this recipe tends to vary in different communities, as does the cooking time. Some families say, 'Dal ko galne do' (Let it cook completely), while others prefer to use lentils that hold together but still thicken the resulting Dalcha. My mother belonged to the latter school of thought and used toor dal, but I prefer a basic masoor (red lentil), which disintegrates in the Dalcha and blends brilliantly with the spices, making the lamb the star of the dish.

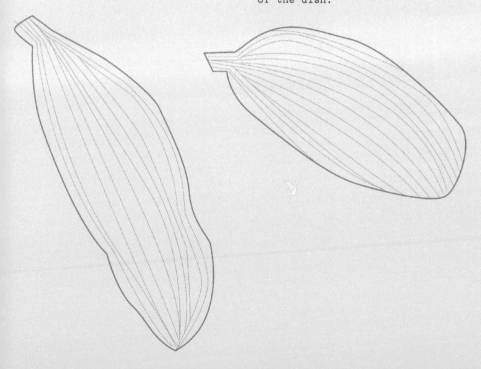

Punjabi Kaali Dal...BLACK LENTIL CURRY
WITH GARLIC, TOMATO AND GINGER

280g whole urad dal
(black lentils),
soaked overnight

60g red kidney beans,
soaked overnight

60g channa dal
(yellow dried split
peas), soaked
overnight

pinch of salt

3 tbsp vegetable oil

pinch of asafoetida

1 green bird's
eye chilli, slit
lengthways

1 tsp coarsely ground
cumin seeds

6 garlic cloves,
finely chopped

1 onion (about 210g),
finely chopped

2 tomatoes (about
220g), finely chopped

3 tbsp tomato purée

2.5cm piece of fresh
root ginger, finely
chopped

1 tsp Kashmiri chilli
powder or mild
paprika

½ tsp garam masala

1 tbsp butter

FOR THE GARNISH

60ml single cream

roughly chopped fresh
coriander

1.5cm piece of fresh
root ginger, cut into
slivers

1 finely chopped green
birds-eye chilli
(optional)

Punjabi-style black lentils are traditionally cooked slowly over coals, but the hob-based version below is equally splendid. The pulses impart a thick creaminess unique to Kaali Dal.

1. Drain the urad dal and kidney beans. Place in a large, heavy-based saucepan with 1.5 litres water. Add a pinch of salt, bring to a boil and simmer over a low heat for 1 hour, stirring from time to time and skimming off the foam from the surface.

2. Drain the channa dal, add to the simmering pan and continue cooking for 1 hour 15 minutes. Drain, reserving the cooking water. Mash the lentils with a potato masher. (This will take some armwork, so keep going till they have a coarse consistency — you want most of them mashed, but some left whole.)

3. Place a large heavy-based saucepan over a low heat and add the oil. When hot, add the asafoetida, bird's eye chilli and cumin seeds. Let them sizzle for 5 seconds and add the garlic, frying for a further 20 seconds.

4. Now turn the heat to medium and add the onions. Fry for 7—10 minutes until they begin to soften, stirring well to make sure they don't stick to the pan. Add the tomatoes and fry for 2 minutes, mashing them with the back of the spoon when softened. Add the purée and cook for 1 minute.

5. Add the ginger and fry for a minute, then add the chilli powder. Season to taste and add the mashed dal. Stir well, making sure the spices are thoroughly mixed with the dal. Add 650ml of the reserved cooking liquid and stir. Bring to a boil and simmer, covered, over a low heat for 20—25 minutes, stirring continually to prevent the mixture from sticking to the bottom of the pan. (The dal should be thick and creamy, so add a touch more water only if you need to.)

6.Add the garam masala and butter and stir well, simmering for a minute. Just before serving, garnish with a swirl of cream, the fresh coriander and ginger. (If you'd like it slightly spicy, add the chilli too.) Serve with naan or chapattis.

Malwani Chicken Masala

2 tbsp vegetable oil

pinch of asafoetida

1 onion (about 120g), thinly sliced

3 tbsp Malwani Masala (page 248)

1kg chicken on the bone, cut into medium-sized pieces (ask your butcher)

salt to taste

FOR THE COCONUT PASTE

1 red onion (about 40g), chopped

200g freshly grated coconut

3 green bird's eye chillies

5 garlic cloves

2.5cm piece of fresh root ginger

FOR THE GARNISH

2 tbsp lemon juice

2 tbsp finely chopped fresh coriander

This chicken curry, from the Malwani region of western India, is made with a unique spice blend that traditionally includes dagad phool. This isn't readily available in the UK, but my Malwani spice blend (full recipe on page 248) is based around a family recipe I have used since living in the UK, and gives the traditional Malwani gravy flavour. Cooked with fresh coconut, this warming dish is ideal with dosas (soft flatbreads made with ground rice).

1. First make the coconut paste, put all the ingredients for it in a blender with 50ml water and blitz to a thick paste.

2. Place a heavy-based pan over a medium heat and add the oil. When hot, add the asafoetida; let it sizzle for a couple of seconds, then add the sliced onion. Cook over a medium heat, stirring occasionally, for about 7 minutes until softened and light brown. Now add the coconut paste. Stir well, lower the heat and cook for 5–7 minutes or until the coconut changes colour slightly to a pale brown. (Stir occasionally to make sure it doesn't stick to the bottom of the pan.)

3. Now add 3 tablespoons of the Malwani masala and fry for 1 minute. Add the chicken and cook over a medium heat for 3 minutes, coating all the pieces with the coconut and spices. Add 500ml water, season and mix. Bring the curry to a boil and simmer gently, covered, for 25 minutes or until the chicken is cooked through, stirring well a couple of times during cooking. Partly cover with a lid and simmer for a further 8 minutes.

4. Sprinkle over the lemon juice and fresh coriander and serve with dosas or your choice of Indian bread.

Keralan Kozhi Kuttan...CHICKEN CURRY
WITH CHILLIES AND COCONUT MILK

½ tsp ground turmeric

1 tbsp Greek yoghurt, lightly whisked

800g chicken, skinned and jointed

3 tbsp vegetable oil

2 green bird's eye chillies, slit lengthways

1 onion (about 170g), thinly sliced

2 tomatoes (about 140g total weight), puréed to a smooth paste

100ml thick coconut milk

salt to taste

pinch of red chilli flakes or chopped fresh coriander to garnish

FOR THE PASTE

1 tbsp vegetable oil

2.5cm piece of fresh root ginger, roughly chopped

8 garlic cloves

1 tbsp coriander seeds

4 dried Kashmiri chillies (or any dried mild red chillies)

2 heaped tsp fennel seeds

½ tsp black peppercorns

4cm cassia bark

5 green cardamom pods, seeds only

This Keralan-style chicken dish ('kozhi' means chicken) includes an amalgamation of spices that go to make a gorgeous curry paste I quite often use for lamb as well as chicken. Coconut oil is traditionally used in this dish and it does add richness, but regular vegetable oil works just as well. The use of coconut milk is quite minimal and serves merely to thicken the sauce and add a creamier flavour — a little goes a long way.

1. Put the turmeric, yoghurt and a pinch of salt in a bowl and mix well. Add the chicken pieces and leave to marinate for an hour or so.

2. Meanwhile, make the paste. Place a frying pan over a low heat and add the oil, followed by the ginger and garlic. Fry for about 1 minute, then add the rest of the paste ingredients and fry for 5—6 minutes until lightly coloured. Leave to cool, then put the mixture in a blender, add 50—70ml water and blitz to a fine paste. Set aside.

3. Place a heavy-based non-stick pan over a medium heat and add the 3 tablespoons of oil. When hot, add the bird's eye chillies, letting them sizzle for about 10 seconds. Tip in the onion, add a pinch of salt and fry for 10—12 minutes or until browned. Add the puréed tomatoes and stir well, cooking for 3 minutes. Now add the spice paste and fry for 4—5 minutes stirring well, until the sauce thickens slightly and the oil leaves the sides of the pan.

4. Now turn the heat up slightly and add the marinated chicken pieces, stirring well to coat them with the spice paste. Fry for 4 minutes until lightly coloured. Add 100ml water and season to taste. Simmer, covered, for 25 minutes until the chicken is cooked through.

5. Add the coconut milk, stir well and simmer for a further 5—7 minutes or until the sauce is slightly thickened. Garnish with the chilli flakes or coriander and serve with Apple and Fennel Raita (see page 241) and parathas.

Chicken Ishtew... SOUTH INDIAN CHICKEN AND COCONUT STEW

4–5 garlic cloves

2 tbsp vegetable oil

1 tbsp butter

2cm cassia bark

5 cloves

6–7 green cardamom pods

1 onion (about 180g), thinly sliced

1 green bird's eye chilli, slit lengthways

1 potato (about 140g), cubed

1 tomato (about 100g), roughly chopped

1 x 900g chicken, skinned, jointed and cut into small pieces (ask your butcher to do this)

2 tsp coarsely ground black pepper

250ml coconut milk

80g frozen green peas

pinch of sugar

salt to taste

FOR THE GARNISH

1.5cm piece of fresh root ginger, thinly sliced

1 tbsp roughly chopped fresh coriander

10 fresh curry leaves

A south Indian-inspired stew that's perfect for cosy nights in. With its flavours of curry leaves, ginger, chillies and coconut milk, this warming bowl packs a punch and is something I cook to ward off colds and flu too.

1. Put the garlic into a blender, add a little water and blitz to a paste. Set aside.

2. Place a deep sauté pan over a medium heat and add the oil and butter. When hot, add the cassia bark, cloves and cardamom pods and fry until the spices crackle.

3. Add the onion and cook for 7–8 minutes on a medium heat. Add the bird's eye chilli and the garlic paste and fry for a further minute, adding a splash of water (2 tablespoons) if it sticks to the bottom of the pan. Add the potato and fry for 2 minutes, then add the tomato. Stir well and mash with the back of the spoon. They will begin to soften after a minute.

4. Add the chicken pieces and mix well, frying them for 6–7 minutes to seal on all sides. Add 150ml water and bring to a boil, then simmer, covered, over a low heat for 20–25 minutes or until the chicken is cooked, stirring halfway through cooking.

5. Pour in the coconut milk and the green peas and let the stew simmer away for a further 5 minutes.

6. Season to taste, add the sugar and garnish with the ginger. Just before serving, add the coriander and curry leaves. Serve with dosas, rice or chapattis.

Chukhandar ka Gosht...BEETROOT
AND LAMB CURRY

6 garlic cloves

2.5cm piece of fresh root ginger

800g lamb on the bone, cut into bite-sized pieces (ask your butcher to do this)

2 tbsp Greek yoghurt

350g cooked beetroot (shop-bought variety is fine, but not the ones in vinegar!)

3 tbsp vegetable oil

5 green cardamom pods

2 bay leaves

2.5cm cassia bark, broken in half

5—6 cloves

1 red onion (about 180g), thinly sliced

1½ tsp Kashmiri chilli powder or mild paprika

2 tsp ground coriander

½ tsp garam masala

salt to taste

FOR THE GARNISH
generous handfuls of roughly chopped fresh coriander and mint

1.5cm piece of fresh root ginger, cut into slivers

1 tbsp lemon juice

This beetroot and lamb dish is an authentic north Indian curry. I first ate it at a friend's place a few years back — her family are Muslim, and this meat curry is probably one of my favourites from that community. Chukhandar, or beetroot, is cooked with the moist tender lamb, rendering a sweetness to the dish amidst the warmth of the spices and the hit of chilli, as well as a stunning red colour.

1. Put the garlic and ginger into a blender, add a splash of water and blitz to a smooth paste. Place in a bowl and add the lamb and yoghurt. Mix well and leave to marinate for a few hours or preferably overnight.

2. Put the beetroot in a blender and blitz to a coarse paste.

3. When ready to cook, place a heavy-based saucepan over a medium heat and add the oil. When hot, add the cardamom pods, bay leaves, cassia and cloves. Fry for 20—30 seconds, then add the sliced red onion and fry for 8—10 minutes until it begins to soften and turn light brown.

4. Add the lamb and its marinade to the pan. Stir well and add the chilli powder and ground coriander. Mix the spices with the meat and seal the pieces for 5—7 minutes. Add 300ml water, bring to a boil, season and simmer for 45 minutes, stirring halfway through cooking.

5. Add the beetroot paste and simmer for a further 15 minutes, then add the garam masala, remove from the heat and leave to stand for 5 minutes. Garnish with the coriander, mint, ginger and lemon juice and serve with Simple Pulao and Pineapple Raita (see pages 235 and 238).

Salli Kheema Pav...MINCED LAMB WITH CHILLI AND COCONUT

4 garlic cloves

1.5cm piece of fresh root ginger

800g minced lamb

2 tbsp vegetable oil

5–7 fresh curry leaves

2 onions (about 190g total weight), finely chopped

2 tomatoes (about 180g total weight), finely chopped

2 green bird's eye chillies, finely chopped

1 tbsp finely chopped fresh coriander

1 heaped tsp Kashmiri chilli powder or mild paprika

½ tsp ground turmeric

180ml coconut milk

1 tsp dark brown sugar

2 tbsp malt vinegar

salt to taste

FOR THE SPICE POWDER

3 green cardamom pods

1 blade of mace

2.5cm cassia bark

½ star anise

3 cloves

4–5 black peppercorns

When I was growing up in India, kheema, or minced lamb, slow-cooked in spices and garnished with fresh coriander and salli (crisp potato straws) was always served with what we called a 'laadi pav' (buttie). The melt-in-your-mouth spiced kheema had a hint of zingy lemon cutting through the heat and richness of the dish...that's how I remember it, and exactly what this recipe delivers.

1. First make the spice powder. Put all the ingredients for it into a spice or coffee grinder, blitz to a fine powder and set aside.

2. Blend the ginger and garlic to a fine paste. Place in a bowl, add the lamb and mix well. Set aside while you get started on the curry.

3. Place a heavy-based saucepan over a medium heat and add the oil. When hot, add the curry leaves and let them sizzle. Tip in the onions and fry for 5–7 minutes until softened and light brown. Now add the chopped tomatoes and fry over a medium heat, cooking for a further 5 minutes until they are soft enough to be mashed slightly with the back of your spoon.

4. Add the bird's eye chillies, chopped coriander, chilli powder and turmeric. Stir well to cook the spices for a couple of minutes, then add the marinated lamb. Keep stirring over a medium heat and break down the lamb to make sure there are no lumps when mixing in all the spices. Cook for 5 minutes and then add 100ml water. Bring to a boil, cover and simmer — you want the lamb to cook for 20 minutes or so until it's absorbed almost all the water.

Continued overleaf

5. Now add the coconut milk and the spice powder. Simmer for a further 5—7 minutes, half-covered with a lid, then add the sugar, vinegar and salt. Stir well. Remove the lid and cook for a further 5 minutes.

6. Meanwhile, make the salli. Heat a deep-fat fryer to 170°C or fill a large saucepan or kadhai (deep wok) one-third full of oil and heat until a cube of bread dropped into the hot oil sizzles and turns golden brown in 30 seconds. Dab the potato straws with kitchen paper to get rid of as much moisture as possible. Add them to the hot oil and deep-fry them for 1—2 minutes, until golden brown. Remove and drain on kitchen paper. Sprinkle with some salt.

7. Serve the lamb garnished with the coriander, lemon juice and potato straws. Offer pav or lightly fried soft butties, and a red onion salad on the side.

TIP
● ● ● ● ● ●

To avoid the hassle of chopping and frying the potato straws, I sometimes buy ready-made ones, which are readily available in the shops.

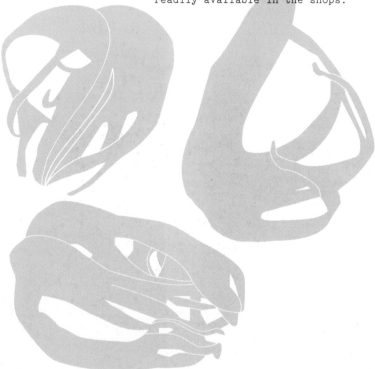

Bengali Kosha Mangsho...MARINATED LAMB
CURRY WITH MUSTARD, YOGHURT AND SPICES

3 tbsp Greek yoghurt

¼ tsp ground turmeric

1 tbsp mustard oil (optional)

800g leg of lamb on the bone, cut into 4cm pieces (ask your butcher to do this)

3 garlic cloves

2.5cm piece of fresh root ginger

3 tbsp vegetable oil

4 green cardamom pods

5 cloves

1.5cm cassia bark

2 dried mild Kashmiri chillies

1 onion (about 120g), finely sliced

1 heaped tbsp tomato purée

2 tsp ground coriander

1 tsp ground cumin

1 tsp Kashmiri chilli powder or mild paprika

1 potato (about 150g), cut into chunks

1 tbsp lemon juice

salt to taste

1 tbsp roughly chopped fresh coriander to garnish

This family recipe comes from a very dear Bengali friend of my grandmother's. They both shared a love for cooking and eating, and would often exchange recipes, even planning on putting a book together in the 1960s. In this dry-fry dish, lamb is cooked in whole spices with dried chillies, resulting in beautifully tender meat that is coated in a lusciously thick masala gravy.

1. Put the yoghurt, turmeric and mustard oil into a mixing bowl. Add a pinch of salt and whisk lightly. Add the lamb, mix well and marinate for 1 hour or preferably overnight.

2. Put the garlic and ginger into a blender or food processor. Add 2 tablespoons of water and blitz to a fine purée. Set aside.

3. When ready to cook the lamb, place a heavy-based saucepan over a medium heat and add the oil. When hot, add the cardamom pods, cloves, cassia bark and dried chillies. Let them sizzle for about a minute to infuse the oil, then add the onion and fry over a medium heat for 10 minutes until it softens and starts to change colour.

4. Add the ginger and garlic paste and fry for 30 seconds. Add the tomato purée and fry for a further minute. Now add all the lamb pieces along with the marinade and, stirring well, seal them for 4–5 minutes over a medium heat. Add the ground coriander, cumin and chilli powder and fry for a further 6–8 minutes. (As the lamb cooks it will start to release its moisture.)

5. Add the potato chunks, season to taste and simmer, covered, for 1 hour until the lamb is tender and cooked through. Stir occasionally during cooking, and a few times towards the end, to make sure it doesn't stick to the bottom of the pan. The gravy should be really thick for this mangsho and cling to the lamb chunks.

6. Add the lemon juice and salt, then garnish with the fresh coriander. Serve warm with puris.

Kheema Aloo Tikki...SPICY LAMB
POTATO CAKES

MAKES 5-6 CAKES

2 green bird's eye
chillies

4 garlic cloves

2.5cm piece of fresh
root ginger

2 tsp ground
coriander

2 tbsp malt vinegar

½ tsp coarsely ground
black pepper

3 tbsp vegetable oil

2 green cardamom pods

1 bay leaf

1 red onion (about
80g), finely chopped

2 tbsp tomato purée
or 3 tbsp tomato
ketchup

½ tsp Kashmiri chilli
powder or mild
paprika

400g leg of lamb,
minced

80g frozen green peas

½ tsp garam masala

salt to taste

roughly chopped
coriander

1 green bird's eye
chilli, finely chopped

This is an absolute family favourite — my mother would use left-over kheema (minced meat) stuffed in potato coated in breadcrumbs and fried until crisp. Served like this, with the simple addition of some ketchup, it is probably the most common snack in Mumbai.
I have added a recipe for making a dry-fry kheema, which is different from usual kheema recipes, as I thought this would be ideal for the patties.

1. Pound the chillies, garlic and ginger to a fine-ish paste using a pestle and mortar. Once the paste starts to come together, mix in the ground coriander, vinegar and black pepper, then set aside.

2. Place a deep sauté pan over a medium heat and add the oil. When hot, add the cardamom pods and bay leaf and let them sizzle for a couple of seconds to infuse the oil.

3. Add the onion and fry for about 8 minutes until softened and light brown in colour. Add the tomato purée and fry for a couple of minutes until the oil leaves the sides of the pan. Stir well, making sure to scrape up anything that sticks to the pan.

4. Add the spicy paste along with the Kashmiri chilli powder and fry for 2 minutes, then add the lamb mince. Turn the heat up slightly and fry for 5 minutes, making sure the masala blends in well and is coloured all over. Add 80ml water and season to taste.

5. Simmer and cook, covered, for 20 minutes, then remove the lid and continue simmering for a further 30 minutes, stirring occasionally. Stir through the peas and garam masala and cook gently until the mixture is dry. Remove from the heat and add the chopped coriander and chilli. Mix well and leave to cool while you prepare the potato mix.

Continued opposite

FOR THE POTATO MIX

4 potatoes (about 500g), boiled

1 slice of white bread

1 heaped tbsp cornflour

1 tbsp finely chopped fresh coriander

oil for shallow-frying

90g plain flour

2 eggs, lightly beaten

90g breadcrumbs

6. Grate the boiled potatoes coarsely in a mixing bowl. Soak the bread in a little cold water for a few seconds, then squeeze out any excess moisture. Transfer it to the bowl with the potatoes and add the cornflour, coriander and some salt. Knead well and refrigerate for 10–15 minutes.

7. When ready, divide the potato mix into 5-6 equal portions. Taking one portion, flatten the potato in the palm of your hand and press down in the centre to create a hollow. Add 2 teaspoons of the lamb mixture and fold the potato over the filling to enclose it and form a patty. If any of the filling spills out, just cover it with the starchy potato mix using your hands. (This is the messy part of the process but very worth it!) Scrape any leftovers from your hands with the fork and mix it into the potato. Make all the patties in the same way and refrigerate for a further 20 minutes.

8. Place a frying pan over a medium to high heat and pour in enough oil to come halfway up the sides. When hot, dip each patty first in the plain flour, then the beaten eggs and finally the breadcrumbs, then fry for 2–3 minutes on each side, making sure they are evenly coloured, crisp and golden brown.

9. Serve with a squeeze of lemon juice and some ketchup in tow.

Punjabi Chole...CHICKPEA CURRY WITH GINGER, POMEGRANATE AND TEA

350g dried chickpeas, soaked in water overnight

80g channa dal (yellow dried split chickpeas)

1 strong teabag

½ tsp bicarbonate of soda

2 tsp cumin seeds

8 garlic cloves

2.5cm piece of fresh root ginger

1 green bird's eye chilli

3 tomatoes (about 260g total weight)

3 tbsp vegetable oil

pinch of asafoetida

2 onions (about 240g total weight), thinly sliced

1 tsp Kashmiri chilli powder or mild paprika

2 heaped tsp ground coriander

3 tsp pomegranate powder (see Tip overleaf)

½ tsp black salt

pinch of sugar

salt to taste

1 tsp dried fenugreek leaves, crushed

½ tsp garam masala

I cook my spicy chickpea curry the same way my mother does, and most Indian households will have their own take on it. Her recipe is from a very dear Punjabi friend who gave us the key to getting that deep rich colour and flavour — always add a teabag while cooking the chickpeas. This is a very common practice in Punjabi households in India, lending a rich smoky flavour to the curry in addition to a deep colour, which enhances the overall result of the dish.

1. Drain the chickpeas and place in a saucepan with the channa dal and about 2 litres of water. Bring to a boil, simmer and cook for 1 hour until they are tender. Make sure to skim the foam off the top as the pulses begin to cook.

2. Add the teabag and simmer, covered, over a low heat for a further 20 minutes. Add the bicarbonate of soda and cook for another 10 minutes, stirring well. Drain, reserving the cooking liquid and discard the teabag. Set the cooking liquid aside. Mash a few of the chickpeas and lentils with a potato masher and set aside.

3. Dry-roast the cumin seeds in a frying pan for 2 minutes. Turn off the heat as they start to release their warm spiced aromas then, using a pestle and mortar or a coffee grinder, crush to a coarse powder and set aside.

4. Blend the garlic, ginger and bird's eye chilli to a fine paste in a wet grinder or mini food processor with a little water. Set aside. Blend the tomatoes to a pulp separately and set aside.

5. Place a heavy-based saucepan over a low heat and add the oil. When hot, add the asafoetida and, as it begins to sizzle, turn up the heat, add the onions and cook over a medium heat for 10 minutes. Stir frequently and as they start to change colour tip in the garlic, ginger and chilli paste. Fry for a minute then add the blended tomatoes and fry for 8–9 minutes until the sauce begins to thicken.

Continued overleaf

FOR THE GARNISH

1 tbsp lemon juice

roughly chopped fresh
coriander

slivers of fresh
root ginger

6. Add the chilli powder, ground coriander and the crushed cumin, and stir for 2 minutes, cooking the spices through. Add the chickpeas, pomegranate powder, black salt and sugar and mix well. Add 700ml of the reserved cooking liquid and season to taste (sparingly as the curry includes black salt).

7. Bring the curry to a boil, then simmer, covered, for a further 30 minutes. Stir a couple of times during cooking to make sure the gravy has thickened but does not stick to the bottom of the pan (add a little more water if you feel it's too thick). Sprinkle in the fenugreek leaves and garam masala, then turn off the heat and garnish with the lemon juice, fresh coriander and slivers of ginger.

8. Serve this chickpea curry warm with deep-fried puris.

TIP
. . . . . .

I have included dried pomegranate powder for an extra tang, although it would be fine to leave it out and just add a touch more lemon.

Bengali Bhapa Maach...STEAMED FISH WITH
MUSTARD AND GREEN CHILLI PASTE

800g fish steaks
(salmon or halibut
would be good)
juice of ½ lemon
½ tsp ground turmeric
salt to taste

FOR THE PASTE
1 tbsp yellow mustard
seeds
2 tbsp black/brown
mustard seeds
80ml warm water
2 green bird's eye
chillies
4 tbsp freshly
grated coconut, or
desiccated coconut
soaked for 2 minutes
in warm water and
drained
pinch of sugar
½ tsp Kashmiri chilli
powder or mild
paprika
½ tsp ground turmeric

In this recipe steamed fish steaks are cooked in a traditional Bengali paste with ground mustard, green chilli and turmeric. The flavours are pungent and seep into the moist fish really well. Commonly eaten with some fluffy rice, this is the ultimate home-cooked comfort food for most Bengalis. Traditionally, ilish (also known as hilsa — a member of the herring family local to eastern India) would be the fish of choice, but salmon works as a brilliant alternative as its oiliness complements the spice flavours really well.

1. First make the paste. Put both types of mustard seeds in a bowl, and soak in the warm water for 30 minutes to soften.

2. While the seeds are soaking, put the fish steaks into a separate bowl and add the lemon juice, turmeric and a pinch of salt. Mix well and leave to marinate for 15—20 minutes.

3. Meanwhile, put the bird's eye chillies, coconut, sugar, chilli powder, turmeric and some salt into a blender. Add the mustard seeds along with half the soaking liquid and blitz to a smooth, fine paste. (Add a little more water only if necessary — you want the paste to be quite thick.) Smear the paste over the fish steaks.

4. Prepare a steamer. If you don't have one, place a trivet covered with an upturned saucer or lid inside a saucepan of water. Make sure the water doesn't touch the bottom of the trivet. Bring the water to a boil.

5. Wrap each fish piece in greaseproof paper and place in the steamer. Cover and steam for 18—20 minutes, until the fish is cooked through. Serve with plain rice.

Kadhi Pakoda...ONION PAKODAS IN SPICED YOGHURT CURRY

50g gram (chickpea)
flour

250g Greek yoghurt

½ tsp ground turmeric

2 tbsp vegetable oil

pinch of asafoetida

1 tsp black/brown
mustard seeds

½ tsp cumin seeds

2 dried chillies

3 garlic cloves,
finely chopped

2.5cm piece of fresh
root ginger, finely
chopped

FOR THE PAKORAS

70g gram (chickpea)
flour

½ tsp ajwain (carom)
seeds

½ tsp ground turmeric

½ tsp Kashmiri chilli
powder or 1 fresh
green bird's eye
chilli, deseeded and
finely chopped

½ tsp baking powder

1 tbsp finely chopped
fresh coriander

1 onion (140g),
halved and thinly
sliced

oil for deep-frying

salt to taste

FOR THE GARNISH

fresh coriander
sprigs

sliced green bird's
eye chillies
(optional)

I love this particular Punjabi recipe because the pakoras are thicker than usual, pack a punch and have a tangy edge to them. Once fried, they are added to the gravy to soak in all the goodness. Comfort in a bowl!

1. First make the pakoras. Put all the ingredients (except the oil) in a bowl and mix well. Now add 50–60ml water a little at a time to make a thick sticky batter. Set aside.

2. Heat a deep-fat fryer to 170°C or fill a large saucepan or kadhai (deep wok) one-third full of oil and heat until a cube of bread dropped into the hot oil sizzles and turns golden brown in 30 seconds. Drop small spoonfuls of batter into the hot oil and let them sizzle until crisp and golden brown all over (see Tip). Drain on kitchen paper.

3. To make the kadhi, put the flour, yoghurt, turmeric and some salt into a bowl and mix well. Add 450ml water and whisk until smooth.

4. Put a heavy-based saucepan over a medium heat and add the oil. When hot, add the asafoetida, mustard seeds and cumin seeds. Let them sizzle to infuse the oil. Add the dried chillies and fry for 2–3 seconds. Now add the garlic and ginger and sauté for a minute on a medium heat.

5. Tip in the yoghurt mixture and stir constantly so it doesn't stick to the pan or split (your kadhi should be creamy). Simmer for 8–10 minutes, stirring halfway through. (The longer it's heated, the more it will thicken, so add a little more water if it starts to thicken too much.)

6. Check the seasoning. Garnish with coriander or a few green bird's eye chillies if liked. Top with the pakoras and serve some rice alongside.

TIP
......

The batter consistency is thick, so it's best to make small pakoras, which ensures they cook well on the inside as well as the outside.

Sindhi Dal Pakwan...SPICED LENTIL, TAMARIND AND CHILLI CURRY WITH CRISPY FLATBREAD

200g channa dal (yellow dried split peas)

½ tsp ground turmeric

2 tbsp vegetable oil

2 onions (about 150g total weight), finely chopped

2 green bird's eye chillies, slit lengthways

1 tomato (about 100g), chopped

½ tsp ground cumin

½ tsp ground coriander

½ tsp kashmiri chilli powder or mild paprika

¼ tsp garam masala

2 tsp tamarind paste

½ tsp amchoor (dry mango powder — optional)

2 tbsp finely chopped fresh coriander

1 red onion (about 70g), finely chopped

juice of 1 lime

salt to taste

With such huge regional diversity in India, it's no surprise that our family meals included this utterly scrummy recipe from the Sindhi community. Cooking dal like the Sindhis do is definitely worth trying. This lentil curry is commonly eaten at breakfast with pakwan (a crispy flatbread), some finely chopped onions and a sprinkling of lemon juice. Try it as a perfect Sunday brunch, followed by a siesta. This is what indulging is all about.

1. Put the channa dal in a saucepan with 1 litre of water, and add the turmeric and a pinch of salt. Bring to a boil, then simmer over a low heat for 50 minutes. Remove from the heat and use a potato masher or the back of a spoon to mash the dal roughly to form a coarse mixture. Set aside.

2. Place a heavy-based saucepan over a medium heat and add the oil. When hot, add the onions and fry over a medium heat for 7 minutes until they start to soften. Add the bird's eye chillies, stirring well, then add the chopped tomato and cook for 2–3 minutes. Add the cumin, coriander, paprika and garam masala. Fry for 30 seconds, then pour in the dal. Stir and add the tamarind paste along with some salt. Simmer, covered, over a low heat for 15 minutes, stirring a couple of times during cooking. Remove from the heat, add the amchoor, if using, and the fresh coriander. Set aside.

Continued opposite

FOR THE PAKWAN

(makes 12–15)
300g plain flour
½ tsp coarsely ground
cumin seeds
¼ tsp mild paprika
1 tbsp melted butter
salt to taste
oil for deep-frying

3. To make the pakwan (flatbreads), put the flour, cumin, paprika, butter and salt into a mixing bowl, then add 180ml water a little at a time, kneading to form a smooth, soft dough. Cover with cling film and leave to rest for 10 minutes.

4. Heat a deep-fat fryer to 170°C or fill a large saucepan or kadhai (deep wok) one-third full of oil and heat until a cube of bread dropped into the hot oil sizzles and turns golden brown in 30 seconds.

5. Divide the pakwan dough into 12–15 equal pieces and roll out each one into a disc 12cm in diameter. Prick evenly with a fork (this will ensure that the pakwan goes slightly crispy without fluffing up). Deep-fry the pakwans one at a time for 2–3 minutes on each side until golden brown. Drain on kitchen paper, then cover with foil to keep warm while you make the rest.

6. Serve the dal in a bowl topped with chopped onions and a teaspoon of lime juice. Eat with the crispy pakwan.

TIP
. . . . . .

Soaking the dal before cooking, even for 20 minutes, will reduce the cooking time. The amchoor (dry mango powder) adds a tart, tangy flavour to the dal. If you don't have any, add a touch more tamarind paste instead.

Rajma Chawal... SLOW-COOKED KIDNEY BEANS WITH CUMIN, GINGER AND CHILLI

300g dried red kidney beans, soaked overnight

60g channa dal (yellow dried split peas)

½ tsp bicarbonate of soda

3 tbsp vegetable oil

1½ tsp cumin seeds

2 dried Kashmiri chillies or mild chillies

4cm cassia bark

2 onions (about 200g total weight), finely chopped

2 green bird's eye chillies, finely chopped

190g tinned chopped tomatoes

5cm piece of fresh root ginger, thinly sliced

¼ tsp ground turmeric

2 tsp ground coriander

¼ tsp garam masala

2 tsp pomegranate powder

salt to taste

2 tbsp chopped fresh coriander and 1 tsp butter to garnish

A famous north Indian kidney bean curry, this is comfort in a bowl. Slow-cooking the beans, combined with the flavours of ginger, chilli and cumin, yields a deliciously creamy gravy.

1. Drain the kidney beans, place them in a large saucepan with the channa dal and add about 1.5 litres water. Bring to a boil, simmer and cook for 1 hour or until tender (make sure to skim the foam off the top as the pulses begin to cook). Simmer for a further 20 minutes on a low heat, add the bicarbonate of soda, stir well and cook for a further 10 minutes. Drain and reserve the cooking liquid. Mash a few of the kidney beans and lentils with a potato masher and set aside.

2. Place a heavy-based saucepan over a medium heat and add the oil. When hot, add the cumin seeds, dried chillies and cassia bark, frying for 20 seconds. Now add the onions and fry for 8—9 minutes, stirring until they soften and begin to turn light brown. Add the bird's eye chillies and fry for a minute before adding the tomatoes. Cook for 3 minutes, then add the ginger and fry for a further 2 minutes — the base sauce will thicken slightly.

3. Add the turmeric and ground coriander and stir for a few seconds. Add the drained mashed kidney beans and channa dal. Stir well, add 525ml of the reserved cooking liquid and season to taste. Bring to a boil and simmer over a low heat for 30 minutes, stirring from time to time to make sure the mixture doesn't stick to the bottom of the pan.

4. Add the garam masala and pomegranate powder then remove from the heat and garnish with fresh coriander and butter. Serve with Burani Raita (see page 240).

Dal Dhokli...INDIAN-STYLE PASTA WITH TANGY LENTIL CURRY

200g toor dal (split pigeon peas)

1.4 litres warm water

pinch of ground turmeric

pinch of salt

2 tbsp vegetable oil

pinch of asafoetida

1 tsp black/brown mustard seeds

½ tsp cumin seeds

4 cloves

2.5cm cassia bark, broken in half

1 onion (about 80g), thinly sliced

2 green bird's eye chillies, slit lengthways

12 fresh curry leaves

1 tbsp grated ginger (6cm piece of fresh root ginger)

½ tsp ground turmeric

½ tsp Kashmiri chilli powder or mild paprika

2 tsp tamarind paste

2 tbsp jaggery or soft brown sugar

salt

This Gujarati lentil curry is made with a gram flour-based pasta (dhokli) to soak up all the sweet and sour flavours. It takes time to put together, but it's so worth it to have a bowlful of this steaming warm, sweet and sour lentil curry to tuck into.

1. Put the dal in a small saucepan with the warm water, turmeric and salt. Bring to a boil and simmer for 45–50 minutes until it's cooked all the way through. Leave to cool slightly, then mash to a coarse consistency using a hand blender or potato masher — it shouldn't be too smooth. Set aside.

2. To make the dhokli, mix 2 tablespoons of the oil with the rest of the ingredients for it in a bowl, adding 100ml water if needed, and knead to a smooth dough. Cover with cling film and set aside.

3. Place a heavy-based saucepan over a medium heat and add the oil. When hot, add the asafoetida and mustard seeds, letting them splutter for a few seconds, followed by the cumin seeds. Fry for 10 seconds, then add the cloves and cassia bark, frying for a further 30 seconds. Add the sliced onion and fry for 6–7 minutes until it begins to soften and go light brown.

4. Now add the bird's eye chillies and most of the curry leaves, reserving some to garnish. Stir for a few seconds and add the ginger. Fry for 30 seconds, stirring well to make sure it doesn't stick to the bottom of the pan. Add the powdered spices and stir well for a few seconds.

5. Tip in the cooked dal and stir well. Add the tamarind paste and jaggery. Stir well to mix it in, then season to taste. Bring to a boil and simmer gently over a low heat for 7–8 minutes.

Continued opposite

FOR THE DHOKLI
(strips of gram flour dough)

125g wholemeal flour or plain flour

2 tbsp gram (chickpea) flour

½ tsp Kashmiri chilli powder or mild paprika

½ tsp ground turmeric

½ tsp ajwain (carom) seeds

4 tbsp vegetable oil

salt to taste

FOR THE GARNISH

chopped fresh coriander

1 red onion (about 60g), finely chopped

juice of 1 lemon

6. While the dal is simmering, knead the dhokli dough well, then divide it into 4 equal portions. Pour 2 tablespoons of oil into a bowl. Dab some onto each piece of dough, then roll them out to a width of 15cm. Using a pizza cutter or knife, cut the dough into strips about 2.5cm wide. (They'll be different lengths, but that doesn't matter.)

7. Now add 200ml warm water to the dal and simmer for a minute. Add the dhokli strips one at a time to the dal, stirring gently to make sure they don't stick to the bottom. Cook for 12–15 minutes, stirring a few times during cooking, and only adding a little more water if the dal is too thick.

8. Turn off the heat and serve warm. Ladle the curry into bowls and top with the fresh coriander, a little red onion and some lemon juice. If you're feeling really decadent, top with some butter too!

TIP
••••••

Adjust the quantities of tamarind and jaggery based on the flavour balance you prefer. Personally, I like a really tangy, sweet-flavoured dal, so I add a touch more jaggery. Also, the longer the dhokli cooks in the dal, the thicker the dal will get, so if you feel the consistency needs to be thinned out, add some more water just before serving.

South Indian Kheer...COCONUT RICE PUDDING

160ml full-fat milk

50g basmati rice

40g jaggery or
unrefined brown sugar

5 cardamom pods,
seeds only, pounded
to a fine powder

300ml coconut milk

TO SERVE

2 tsp butter

1 tbsp roughly
chopped cashew nuts

1 tbsp roughly
chopped pistachios

1 tbsp raisins

pinch of saffron

Coconut rice pudding, also known as 'payasam' in south India, is full of flavour, decadent and almost always makes me go for second helpings! A hint of cardamom, jaggery and coconut milk in the humble pudding is what really lifts the flavour. Topped with fried cashew nuts and puffy raisins, it is a mouthful of gorgeousness. The south Indian version is similar to the northern one, but (unlike my recipe) is traditionally made with short-grain rice and is a tad milkier in consistency.

1. Heat the milk in a wide, heavy-based saucepan until it comes to a rolling boil. Add the rice and simmer for 5–7 minutes, stirring frequently. Add the jaggery and ground cardamom seeds and stir for a further 3 minutes to dissolve.

2. Keeping the heat low, add the coconut milk and stir well to mix. Simmer for a further 20 minutes until it thickens and goes creamy, stirring to make sure it doesn't stick to the bottom of the pan. Remove from the heat and leave to cool, covered with a lid.

3. To serve, heat the butter in a frying pan over a low heat and add the cashew nuts. Brown slightly, then add the pistachios and raisins and fry for a few seconds. Pour this mixture over the pudding, sprinkle with the saffron and serve warm.

Cheat's Ras Malai...MILK DUMPLINGS IN SWEET SAFFRON AND CREAM SYRUP

1.2 litres full-fat milk

5 green cardamom pods

generous pinch of saffron

1 x 397g can condensed milk

handful of roughly chopped pistachios and almonds to garnish

FOR THE DUMPLINGS

100g full-fat milk powder

¼ tsp ground cardamom

½ tsp baking powder

1 egg

1 tbsp melted butter

I've included this simplified version of Ras Malai because the original recipe takes forever to make. And if you need that sugar rush (as I always seem to!), then this is the one you can fall back on. It's also a make-ahead dessert that can be chilled until you are ready to serve.

1. Put the milk and cardamom pods in a wide, large saucepan and bring to a rolling boil. Add the saffron and condensed milk, then lower the heat and simmer for 40 minutes, making sure to keep stirring every few minutes and scraping the sides and bottom of the pan so the mixture doesn't stick. The milk will reduce by half and thicken. Remove from the heat while you make the dumplings.

2. Put the milk powder, cardamom and baking powder into a mixing bowl. Make a well in the centre and add the egg along with the butter. Mix and knead to form a smooth dough (there might be a few cracks but that's OK).

3. Bring the milk back to a boil on a low heat. Divide the dumpling dough into 12—14 equal portions (they will be quite small) and add them a few at a time to the pan. Cook them on a low heat for 4 minutes without a lid, they will start to double in size and rise to the top. After 4 minutes, turn them over lightly with a spoon to make sure they are softened — be gentle as they are still quite soft. Now put the lid on and simmer for a further 4 minutes.

4. Remove from the heat and leave to cool slightly. Refrigerate and serve cold, garnished with pistachios and almonds.

Mango and Cardamom Barfi... MANGO, PISTACHIO AND CARDAMOM FUDGE

250g full-fat milk powder
250ml mango purée (see Tip)
100ml condensed milk
100ml double cream
½ tsp ground cardamom
10 pistachios, coarsely chopped

Mango season at home was a feast — and it still is. Whether it's in milkshakes, kulfi or, of course, simply sliced, it's a pleasure to tuck into something that is so gorgeously sweet and addictive. One of my favourite puddings is the traditional milk-based dessert barfi, which, when infused with fresh mango purée, becomes extra yummy and delicious. This recipe is a simple version, which achieves the same results while saving preparation and setting time.

TIP
. . . . . .
Shop-bought purée is fine here. Alternatively, chop the flesh of 2–3 mangoes, put them a blender and blend to a smooth purée. Strain through a sieve before using.

1. Line a shallow 23 x 23cm dish with greaseproof paper.

2. Sift the milk powder to get rid of all the lumps and set aside.

3. Put the mango purée in a small saucepan. Add the condensed milk, mix well and bring to a boil. Simmer, stirring frequently, for 12 minutes until the mixture reduces slightly. Add the double cream and continue cooking for a further 15 minutes. Add the ground cardamom.

4. As the mixture thickens, quickly whisk in the milk powder a few tablespoons at a time. Make sure it is thoroughly blended in. Keep the heat low and continue stirring for a further 15 minutes to ensure there are no lumps. You are aiming for the consistency of a smooth, thick paste.

5. Put the Barfi in the prepared dish, smooth out the edges and sprinkle with the pistachios. Cool and set in the refrigerator for 2–3 hours or preferably overnight. Cut into squares and serve.

CELEBRATORY

Celebrate *verb*
to observe (a day
or event) with
ceremonies of
respect, festivity,
or rejoicing.

So we're upping the ante a bit here and every Indian would agree that food is best shared in amazing company! Cook with your heart and have your family and friends over for the lavish banquet to celebrate that special occasion. Curries that are bold, full of flavour and take centre stage on your dinner table. From the show-stopping MALWANI HIRWA TISRYA MASALA (clams cooked in coriander and coconut, page 192) to one of the dishes that always win me heaps of praise at a dinner party, a CHICKEN REZALA (page 178) cooked in creamy gravy with saffron and pistachio. For me no dinner party is complete without a rice dish so in this chapter I have three, including MALYALI KOZHI BIRYANI (page 175).

The desserts are particularly important in this chapter. GHARGE (page 212) are spiced pumpkin pancakes and I include a family recipe I am particularly proud of. Also a really simple yet classic version of BENGALI BHAPA DOI (page 214) a yoghurt infused dessert with strawberries and cardamom. Stunning and delicious.

The recipes in this chapter are ideal for when you want to plan a bit in advance. Prepare a dinner party for family and friends to savour every minute of your time together. This is exactly how four generations of women in my family did it, and if they were all to see this chapter they would be immensely proud to see what's included. There is a saying in India — no matter how big or small your occasion the most important thing is that people will always remember the food. I suppose my mother taught me well. Celebrate, devour and feast!

All recipes serve 4.

Bharwan Mirchi Pakode...SPICED POTATO CHILLIES

8 long, mild red or green Anaheim peppers (around 20–50g each), or similar mild long chilli peppers

oil for deep-frying

FOR THE FILLING
3 potatoes (about 380g total weight), boiled, peeled and mashed

¼ tsp ajwain (carom) seeds

2 tsp mint chutney or 1 tbsp finely chopped mint and coriander

1 green bird's eye chilli, finely chopped

4cm piece of fresh root ginger, finely grated

¼ tsp mild chilli powder

salt to taste

chaat masala powder (optional) to garnish

FOR THE BATTER
100g gram (chickpea) flour

3 tbsp coarse semolina

½ tsp baking powder

½ tsp ground turmeric

In this recipe mild chilli peppers are stuffed with spicy potatoes, then fried in batter for a crispy coating, and every bite is utterly divine! If you plan on making this part of a finger-food menu, use really small Anaheim peppers, which are mild and perfect for stuffing with the potato.

1. Slit the peppers lengthways down one side and deseed them (make sure to keep them whole).

2. Mix all the filling ingredients and stuff some into each chilli (try not to overfill them, or they might leak while frying). Refrigerate the chillies for 20 minutes or so.

3. To make the batter, put all the ingredients for it in a bowl. Mix well and slowly pour in about 140ml water, whisking constantly to make sure there are no lumps (you want the batter to have the consistency of double cream).

4. Heat a deep-fat fryer to 170°C or fill a large saucepan or kadhai (deep wok) one-third full of oil and heat until a cube of bread dropped into the hot oil sizzles and turns golden brown in 30 seconds. Dip each chilli pepper in the batter, slowly add to the oil and deep-fry for about 5 minutes or until golden brown.

5. Drain on kitchen paper and serve warm with the mint and tamarind chutneys on pages 225 and 222, and a sprinkle of chaat masala, if using.

Malyali Kozhi Biryani...SOUTHERN
INDIAN CHICKEN BIRYANI

850g chicken on the bone, skinned and jointed into small pieces (ask your butcher to do this)

1 heaped tbsp ginger paste (made from a 6cm piece of fresh root ginger)

½ tbsp garlic paste (made from 4 garlic cloves)

4 green bird's eye chillies, ground to a paste

½ tsp ground turmeric

4 tbsp vegetable oil

1 tsp ground black pepper

4 green cardamom pods

2 onions (280g total weight), thinly sliced

10–15 fresh curry leaves

½ tsp Kashmiri chilli powder or mild paprika

1 tsp ground fennel

1 tsp ground coriander

100ml coconut milk

salt to taste

This recipe comes from a Malyali family, and was taken from scrappy pieces of paper handwritten with no specific measurements by the lady of a house on the outskirts of Mumbai fifteen years ago. It's one I've always loved and I still cook it when I have guests. Unlike the regular ingredients found in most biryanis such as saffron or mint, here it's black pepper, fennel and coconut milk that make this dish so flavoursome. The original recipe mentions a traditional local short grain rice that isn't readily available in the UK, so I've replaced it with basmati instead. You are looking for a fluffy biryani of separated grains with the masala coating the chicken pieces. Serve while still warm and let its aromas fill the air — your guests will find it irresistible.

1. Put the chicken in a large bowl. Add half the ginger paste, half the garlic paste and half the chilli paste along with the turmeric. Mix well and marinate for a few hours or preferably overnight.

3. Place a heavy-based saucepan over a medium heat and add the oil. When hot, add the black pepper and green cardamom pods and let them sizzle for a few seconds. Add the onions along with a pinch of salt and fry over a medium heat for about 10 minutes. (Stir frequently, making sure they don't stick to the bottom of the pan.) Add the remaining garlic, ginger and chilli pastes and fry for about 1 minute, stirring well.

4. Add the marinated chicken pieces, curry leaves, chilli powder, ground fennel and coriander, then turn the heat up a little and fry for 5 minutes to seal the meat, stirring and mixing well. Add 100ml water, bring to a boil and simmer over a low heat. Season to taste, cover and cook the chicken for 18 minutes on a low heat, stirring halfway through. Add the coconut milk and simmer for a further 5–7 minutes. Remove from the heat and leave to rest.

Continued overleaf

FOR THE RICE

500g basmati rice

2 bay leaves

5cm cassia bark, broken in half

TO LAYER THE BIRYANI

2 tbsp melted butter

4 tbsp coconut milk

½ tsp garam masala

3 tbsp chopped fresh coriander

FOR THE GARNISH

3 tbsp vegetable oil

2 red onions (about 230g total weight), thinly sliced

pinch of sugar

1 tbsp roughly chopped cashew nuts

1 tbsp raisins

5. Soak the rice for 15 minutes in cold water. Heat 1.5 litres of fresh water in a large saucepan with the bay leaves and cassia bark. Drain the rice before adding it to the saucepan and cook over a medium heat for 18–20 minutes until done but still with a slight bite.

6. When ready to finish the dish, preheat the oven to 180°C/350°F/Gas mark 4.

7. Meanwhile, place a tablespoon of butter in a lidded casserole dish and layer the biryani as follows: start with a quarter of the rice, then add a tablespoon of coconut milk, followed by a third of the chicken along with a little gravy, a pinch of the garam masala and some fresh coriander. Continue layering in this order, making sure to finish with rice as the last layer. Top with the remaining butter and coconut milk.

8. Cover the casserole dish with greaseproof paper and fit with a tight lid. Place in the oven and cook for 18–20 minutes until the rice has absorbed all the flavours, and the grains are separated. Turn off the heat and leave to rest for 10 minutes in the oven.

9. To finish the biryani, place a frying pan over a medium heat and add 2 tablespoons of the oil. When hot, add the red onions and fry for 10 minutes with a pinch of sugar until they begin to colour. Remove from the pan and drain on kitchen paper. Add the remaining oil and fry the cashew nuts and raisins, until the nuts turn light brown and the raisins puff up.

10. Discard all the whole spices from the baking dish and serve the biryani topped with the fried onions, nuts and raisins.

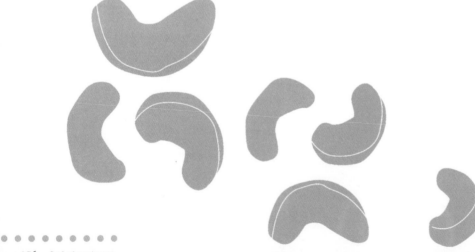

Rajasthani Safed Maas...LAMB CURRY
WITH CARDAMOM, CLOVES AND YOGHURT

80g cashew nuts
3 tbsp vegetable oil
5 dried Kashmiri
chillies (or other
mild dried red
chillies)
4cm cassia bark
1 bay leaf
2 onions (about 190g
total weight), thinly
sliced
5cm piece of fresh
root ginger, grated
800g leg of lamb on
the bone, diced into
bite-sized pieces
(ask your butcher to
do this)
180g Greek yoghurt
½ tsp ground cardamom
(made from the
crushed seeds of 4–5
pods)
1 tsp rose water
salt to taste
1 tbsp chopped fresh
coriander to garnish

Rajasthani people, from the northwest of
India, are famed for their meat curries —
hearty, robust flavours with succulent meat
slow-cooked in a variety of spices. Here Safed
Maas (which means 'white meat') is infused
with cardamom, cloves and natural yoghurt in
a dish that is creamy with a hint of spice.

1. Soak the cashew nuts in enough warm water to
cover for 15 minutes. When ready, put them in a
blender with 2 tablespoons of their soaking liquid
and blitz to a fine purée. Set aside.

2. Place a heavy-based saucepan over a medium
heat and add the oil. When hot, add the chillies,
cassia bark and bay leaf and fry for 20 seconds.
Add the sliced onions and sauté for 9–10 minutes,
stirring frequently until they start to change
colour and brown. Add the ginger and fry for 30
seconds, then add the lamb. Turn up the heat
slightly and fry for 4–5 minutes to seal the meat.

3. Lower the heat and add the yoghurt a little
at a time, stirring well to make sure it doesn't
split. Add 350ml water and bring to a boil, then
season to taste. Simmer, covered, for 45 minutes,
stirring a few times during cooking.

4. Add the cashew nut paste, stir well and
continue to simmer for 15 minutes. Stir from time
to time as the gravy thickens to make sure it
doesn't stick to the bottom of the pan.

5. Remove from the heat and add the ground
cardamom along with the rose water. Garnish with
the coriander and serve with chapattis or Simple
Pulao (see page 235).

Chicken Rezala...CHICKEN IN YOGHURT, CARDAMOM AND GINGER

1 onion (about 120g), roughly chopped

6 garlic cloves, roughly chopped

5cm piece of fresh root ginger, roughly chopped

1kg chicken on the bone, skinned and cut into medium pieces (ask your butcher to do this)

2 tsp ground coriander

150ml Greek yoghurt

FOR THE REZALA GRAVY

2 tbsp melted butter

4 green cardamom pods

2 black cardamom pods

2 bay leaves

10 black peppercorns

4 green bird's eye chillies, slit lengthways

100ml full-fat milk

handful of chopped pistachios

pinch of saffron

salt to taste

Although decadent and delicious, this is one of the simplest recipes you could make for a dinner party. Synonymous with the Muslim community of Calcutta, Rezala is a creamy chicken dish made with yoghurt, cardamom, ginger and rose water. A regal dish with loads of flavour.

1. Put the onion, garlic and ginger in a wet grinder or mini food processor. Add 50ml water and blitz to a smooth paste. Transfer to a bowl.

2. Add the chicken, coriander and yoghurt, mix well and leave to marinate for a few hours or preferably overnight.

3. When ready to cook, start with the gravy. Place a heavy-based saucepan over a low heat and add the butter. When hot, add the cardamom pods, bay leaves and peppercorns, fry for 20 seconds, then add the chicken along with the marinade. Turn the heat up slightly and fry for 6 minutes, making sure to seal the meat. Now turn the heat to a low setting, cover and simmer for 20 minutes. Season to taste.

4. Add the bird's eye chillies and milk, stir well and continue cooking for a further 12 minutes, uncovered, until the sauce has thickened. Stir well and add the chopped pistachios and saffron.

5. Turn off the heat and cover to allow the saffron to infuse the curry. Leave until you're ready to eat, then serve with Simple Pulao (see page 235).

Malai Kofte... VEGETABLE DUMPLINGS IN SPICED TOMATO CURRY

MAKES 12-14 KOFTAS

3-4 potatoes (about 300g total weight), boiled

190g paneer (Indian cottage cheese), finely grated

½ tsp ground turmeric

2.5cm piece of fresh root ginger, finely grated

1 green bird's eye chilli, finely chopped

1 tbsp finely chopped fresh coriander

3 heaped tsp cornflour

1 tbsp raisins

oil for deep-frying

In this classic north Indian dish, vegetarian koftas, or dumplings, are made from spiced potatoes and with paneer (Indian cottage cheese), then steeped in a delicious tomato curry. This is one dish Mum would make so often when we had guests over. It spells celebration in all its decadence, and the resulting curry is a dinner party favourite.

1. Start making the gravy. Put the cashew nuts in a bowl with 50ml warm water and leave to soften for 10-15 minutes.

2. Put the garlic, ginger and 1 whole chilli into a wet grinder or mini food processor. Add a little water and blitz to a paste. Set aside.

3. To make the koftas, coarsely grate the potatoes, mash well until smooth and put them in a large bowl. Add the rest of the kofta ingredients except the oil, and mix well. Knead to a dough-like consistency. Cover with cling film until ready to fry.

4. Put the onion for the gravy into a blender. Add 30-40ml water and blitz to a smooth fine paste. Transfer to a bowl and set aside. Put the tomatoes in the same blender and blitz to a smooth pulp. Transfer to a separate bowl and set aside.

5. Put the cashew nuts in a blender with a few teaspoons of their soaking liquid. Blitz to a paste and set aside.

6. To cook the gravy, place a heavy-based saucepan over a medium heat and add the oil. Add the cloves and cassia bark and fry for 1 minute, then add the slit bird's eye chilli and the onion paste. Fry for 4 minutes, stirring well to make sure the mixture doesn't stick to the bottom of the pan. Add the ginger, garlic and chilli paste and fry for 1-2 minutes. Stir well and add the tomato pulp and the tomato purée. Mix well and cook for 6-7 minutes, until the gravy reduces and goes a deeper red colour.

Continued opposite

FOR THE GRAVY

30g cashew nuts

50ml warm water

8 garlic cloves

2.5cm piece of fresh root ginger, roughly chopped

2 green bird's eye chillies, 1 slit lengthways

1 onion (about 120g), roughly chopped

2 tomatoes (about 200g total weight), roughly chopped

2 tbsp vegetable oil

6 cloves

2.5cm cassia bark, broken in half

2 tbsp tomato purée

½ tsp Kashmiri chilli powder or mild paprika

½ tsp sugar

½ tsp garam masala

salt to taste

chopped fresh coriander to garnish

7. At this stage add the chilli powder and the cashew nut paste. Stir well and cook for a further 2 minutes on a low heat, then add 200ml water and simmer for 2–3 minutes. Add the sugar and garam masala, season to taste and garnish with the coriander. Remove from the heat and cover with a lid to keep warm while you fry the koftas.

8. Divide the kofta mix into 12–14 equal portions, then take a portion in the palm of your hand and roll into a cylindrical shape. Repeat with all the other koftas, making sure they are well kneaded and shaped, or they will fall apart while frying.

9. Heat a deep-fat fryer to 170°C or fill a large saucepan or kadhai (deep wok) one-third full of oil and heat until a cube of bread dropped into the hot oil sizzles and turns golden brown in 30 seconds. Deep-fry the koftas in batches (no more than 2 or 3 at a time) until well browned. Drain on kitchen paper.

10. Serve the koftas with the gravy, along with some rice and raita.

TIP
. . . . . .
If you find the koftas are too soft when frying, add an extra teaspoon of cornflour to the next batch of the mixture and knead well before reshaping to fry.

Batata Vada...DEEP-FRIED SPICED POTATO

MAKES 16-18 VADAS

3 potatoes (about 450g total weight), boiled

1 tsp cumin seeds

4 garlic cloves

2 green bird's eye chillies

10 fresh curry leaves

2 tbsp vegetable oil

pinch of asafoetida

½ tsp ground turmeric

1 tsp lemon juice

roughly chopped fresh coriander

salt to taste

FOR THE BATTER

150g gram (chickpea) flour

pinch of Kashmiri chilli powder or mild paprika

½ tsp ground turmeric

oil for deep-frying

These delicious spiced potato fritters are a popular street snack all over India. They're quick, filling and tasty. How bad can that be? I love serving these crisp little morsels as starters with a chilli sauce or chutney.

1. When the potatoes are slightly cooled, roughly mash them with your hands. The mixture should be very slightly lumpy, like crushed potatoes.

2. Pound the cumin seeds, garlic, chillies and curry leaves to a coarse paste using a pestle and mortar.

3. Place a heavy-based saucepan over a low heat and add the oil. When hot, add the asafoetida; let it sizzle for a couple of seconds, then add the spice paste and fry for 10 seconds to allow it to infuse the oil. Add the turmeric and cook for a couple of seconds, stirring to mix, then add the mashed potato and mix well. Season to taste. Cover and cook for a minute, then remove from the heat and add the lemon juice. Leave to cool and add the fresh coriander.

4. Divide the potato mixture into 16–18 equal portions and roll them into balls. Refrigerate for 15–20 minutes to allow them to firm up.

5. To make the batter, mix together the gram flour along with the powdered spices and salt; add 180ml water, whisking to form a smooth and slightly thick batter with the consistency of double cream.

6. Heat a deep-fat fryer to 170°C or fill a large saucepan or kadhai (deep wok) one-third full of oil and heat until a cube of bread dropped into the hot oil sizzles and turns golden brown in 30 seconds. Dip the potato balls in the batter and deep-fry until they are light brown and crispy on the outside.

7. Drain on kitchen paper and serve with some Sticky Sweet Chilli Dipping Sauce or Red Chilli Coconut Chutney (see page 221 or 224). Yum!

Saas ni Macchi...FISH IN CREAMY GARLIC SAUCE

6 garlic cloves

2 tbsp vegetable oil

1 tbsp butter

1½ tsp cumin seeds, coarsely ground

1 onion (160g), finely chopped

3 tbsp plain flour

550g white fish, cut into steaks with the centre bone intact (cod, haddock or monkfish would be good options)

3 green bird's eye chillies, finely chopped

salt to taste

FOR THE EGG MIX

2 eggs

3 tbsp malt vinegar

2 tbsp caster sugar

FOR THE GARNISH

4 cherry tomatoes, quartered

chopped fresh coriander

TIP
...

Keeping the centre bone intact in the fish will help to hold the flesh together while it cooks.

This favourite Parsi fish dish is cooked in a white sauce with chilli, garlic and onions. Topped with crispy onions and fresh coriander, it is often served at Parsi weddings, and at Zoroastrian ceremonies too.

1. Pound the garlic to a paste using a pestle and mortar, then set aside.

2. Put all the egg mix ingredients in a bowl, stir well and set aside.

3. Place a heavy-based saucepan over a low heat and add the oil and butter. When hot, add the cumin seeds and fry for a couple of seconds. Add the onion and fry for 8–9 minutes or until softened, then add the garlic paste and fry for a further minute.

4. Add the flour and stir well, working quickly as it begins to roast. Stir continuously for 2–3 minutes, making sure there are no lumps and that the flour isn't sticking to the pan. Slowly add 600ml water and keep stirring to get a lump-free white sauce (use a whisk if that's easier). Simmer the sauce for 2 minutes on a low heat.

5. Add the fish steaks to the sauce and simmer, covered, over a low heat for 4 minutes or until the fish is cooked through. Transfer the fish steaks to a bowl and take the sauce off the heat.

6. Slowly add a quarter of the warm gravy to the egg mixture, constantly whisking. Put the saucepan containing the remaining gravy back on a low heat, then stir in the egg mix. Simmer for 6 minutes. Add the chillies and season to taste, stirring continuously as the curry thickens slightly. Now put the fish pieces back in the pan and simmer for 1 minute.

7. Remove from the heat and serve garnished with the chopped tomatoes and fresh coriander. (Mum would also add crispy fried onions.)

Haraa Masalewala Murgh...CORIANDER, TAMARIND AND MINT CHICKEN

2 tbsp vegetable oil

1 tsp cumin seeds

1 onion (160—170g), finely chopped

pinch of sugar

1 green bird's eye chilli, slit lengthways

1 heaped tbsp grated fresh ginger

900g chicken on the bone, skinned and jointed into small pieces (ask your butcher to do this)

juice of ½ lemon

salt to taste

FOR THE SPICE PASTE

60g cashew nuts

8 garlic cloves

2 green bird's eye chillies

60g fresh coriander leaves and stems

40g fresh mint leaves

FOR THE GARNISH

roughly chopped fresh coriander

1.5cm piece of fresh root ginger, cut into julienne strips

Hyderabadi spices and tamarind fried with chicken, garlic and coriander combine here to make a rich gravy that's full of flavour, delicious and more-ish.

1. First make the spice paste. Soak the cashew nuts in enough warm water to cover for 15—20 minutes. When ready, put them in a blender with the rest of the spice paste ingredients and 50ml water. Blitz to a smooth paste and set aside.

2. Place a deep heavy-based pan over a medium heat and add the oil. When hot, add the cumin seeds and let them sizzle for 30 seconds. Add the chopped onions and the sugar, and fry for 12—15 minutes, stirring frequently until the onion starts to soften and go a caramel-brown colour. Add the chilli along with the ginger and fry for 1 minute.

3. Add the spice paste mix and fry for another 2 minutes, stirring well to make sure it doesn't stick to the bottom of the pan. Add the chicken pieces and stir well, making sure they are well coated in the green gravy. Fry for 2—3 minutes to seal. Add 500ml water, season to taste and bring to a boil. Simmer for 25 minutes, stirring halfway through cooking, until the chicken pieces are cooked through and are coated by the masala.

4. Garnish with coriander and some fresh ginger. Serve warm with chapattis or Simple Pulao (see page 235).

Kashmiri Dahi Baingan...KASHMIRI
AUBERGINES

1 tsp Kashmiri chilli powder or mild paprika

1 tsp ground fennel

¼ tsp ground ginger

200g Greek yoghurt

2 aubergines (about 600g total weight), cut lengthways into 20cm slices

5 tbsp vegetable oil

pinch of asafoetida

4 green cardamom pods

pinch of sugar

salt to taste

chopped fresh coriander to garnish

Aubergines are cooked here in the traditional Kashmiri way with yoghurt, fennel and chilli powder, plus some ground ginger for an extra touch of heat.

1. Preheat the oven to 200°C/400°F/Gas mark 6.

2. Put the chilli powder, fennel and ginger in a small bowl. Add 50ml water and stir together to form a paste. Mix well to get rid of any lumps, then set aside.

3. Put the yoghurt into a separate bowl and add 20ml water. Mix well to make it smooth.

4. Place the aubergine strips on a baking tray. Sprinkle over a pinch of salt and 3 tablespoons of the oil and roast for 20 minutes or until the aubergine is nearly cooked.

5. Meanwhile, get the gravy ready. Place a heavy-based saucepan over a low heat and add the remaining 2 tablespoons oil. When hot, add the asafoetida and green cardamom pods and fry for 2–3 seconds.

6. Add the spice paste and stir for a minute. Add the yoghurt a little at a time and let it cook for 5 minutes on a low heat, stirring a couple of times during cooking. Now add the roasted aubergines with the sugar and a little more salt. Simmer, covered, for 2 minutes and make sure all the aubergine pieces are coated evenly.

7. Remove from the heat and garnish with freshly chopped coriander. Serve with naan or Simple Pulao (see page 235).

Keralan Beef Chilli Fry

1 tsp Kashmiri chilli powder or mild paprika

2 tbsp coarse garlic paste (made from 16 garlic cloves)

1 tbsp coarse ginger paste (made from a 9cm piece of fresh root ginger)

5 fresh curry leaves, roughly torn

3 tbsp coconut vinegar or malt vinegar

800g beef, sliced into thin strips

salt to taste

chopped fresh coriander to garnish

FOR THE SPICE POWDER

½ tsp black peppercorns

1½ tbsp fennel seeds

5cm cassia bark

6 cloves

5 green cardamom pods, seeds only

TO FRY

3 tbsp vegetable oil

2 green bird's eye chillies, slit lengthways

15 fresh curry leaves

1 red onion (about 170g), thinly sliced

2 tbsp desiccated coconut

2 tsp tamarind paste

Here is a dry-fry southern Indian beef dish that is rustic and very more-ish. The cooking is done in two parts: first in a dry pan to get rid of all the moisture, and then with curry leaves, coconut and tamarind. Although lengthy, this recipe has to be one of my favourites in the book.

1. Place the chilli powder, garlic and ginger pastes, curry leaves, vinegar and salt in a large bowl and add the beef.

2. Grind all the spice powder ingredients to a fine powder in a spice or coffee grinder and add to the beef. Mix well and leave to marinate for 2–3 hours or preferably overnight.

3. When ready to cook, place a heavy-based saucepan over a medium heat. Add the beef and let it cook without any oil for 30–35 minutes. The beef will release all its moisture and dry out slightly. Remove from the heat and cover.

4. To fry, place a wok or saucepan over a medium heat and add the oil. When hot, add the chillies and, as they begin to splutter, add most of the curry leaves (reserving a few for garnish), quickly followed by the sliced onion. Stir well and fry for 7–8 minutes until the onion starts to soften and change colour slightly.

5. Now add the beef and fry for 2 minutes, stirring well. Add the desiccated coconut and tamarind paste and mix well, frying for a further minute. Garnish with coriander and the reserved curry leaves and serve with parathas or chapattis.

Maharashtrian Fish Kalwan
...SPICED FISH CURRY WITH COCONUT AND TAMARIND

500g firm white fish, cut into 5–6 steaks with the centre bone intact (cod, hake or haddock would be ideal)

¼ tsp ground turmeric

1 tsp malt vinegar

2 tbsp vegetable oil

8–10 fresh curry leaves

1 green bird's eye chilli, slit lengthways

1½ tsp Kashmiri chilli powder or mild paprika

2 tsp tamarind paste

50ml coconut milk

salt to taste

chopped fresh coriander to garnish

FOR THE COCONUT PASTE

100g freshly grated coconut, or desiccated coconut soaked for 2 minutes in warm water and drained

5cm piece of fresh root ginger, roughly chopped

4 garlic cloves, roughly chopped

6 black peppercorns

1 tsp cumin seeds

1 green bird's eye chilli

As a true Maharashtrian and Mumbaikar, I don't think I would be doing this book justice if I didn't include our family's Fish Kalwan recipe. It's a major part of my childhood memories — from shopping in the fish market and watching my mother haggle for the best price with the fisherwomen, to getting all the stock home, cleaning it, freezing the extra and then turning it into a brilliant meal. (You could say it was my 'on the job training'.) This dish is honestly something I can never get enough of. The curry is fiery yet light, and the inclusion of coconut milk as well as desiccated coconut makes it truly special.

1. Put the fish steaks on a plate. Add the turmeric and vinegar with a pinch of salt. Rub the mixture over each piece, coating well, and set aside.

2. To make the coconut paste, put all the ingredients into a blender with 70–80ml water and blitz to a smooth fine paste.

3. Place a large heavy-based saucepan over a medium heat and add the oil. When hot, add the curry leaves and bird's eye chilli. Fry for a few seconds and add the coconut paste along with the chilli powder. Fry for 5–6 minutes, stirring continuously to make sure it doesn't stick to the bottom of the pan. Add the tamarind paste and fry for 30 seconds, then add 400ml water. Mix well, season to taste and simmer over a low heat for 2 minutes.

4. Add the fish steaks and stir well, making sure the curry coats all the pieces. Cover and simmer for 3 minutes until the fish is just cooked and still moist. Add the coconut milk and simmer for 1 minute, then garnish with the coriander. Remove from the heat and leave to rest for a few minutes.

5. Serve the curry with plain rice and Koshimbir salad (see page 236).

Nalli Gosht...SPICED LAMB SHANKS

8 garlic cloves

2.5cm piece of fresh root ginger

1 tsp Kashmiri chilli powder or mild paprika

2 tsp ground coriander

4 small lamb shanks

FOR THE CURRY

5cm cassia bark, broken in half

6 green cardamom pods

5 cloves

12 black peppercorns

2 tbsp vegetable oil

1 tbsp butter

2 onions (about 200g total weight), thinly sliced

2 green bird's eye chillies, slit lengthways

½ tsp Kashmiri chilli powder or mild paprika

1 tsp ground turmeric

2 tsp ground coriander

2 heaped tbsp tomato purée

4 tbsp Greek yoghurt

salt to taste

½ tsp ground nutmeg

1 tbsp rose water

salt to taste

FOR THE GARNISH

chopped fresh coriander

1 tsp lemon juice

This recipe always takes me back to the Mughlai restaurants I've visited in Mumbai, many of them serving up plates of gosht (meat) on the bone (nalli) with spiced gravy. Goat meat, cut into small pieces, is traditionally favoured in India, but using lamb shanks makes this the ideal dinner-party dish. And adding rose water and nutmeg at the end gives it that little extra something.

1. Blend the garlic, ginger and about 20ml water to a fine paste. Transfer to a large bowl, then add the chilli powder and ground coriander. Add the lamb shanks, mix well and leave to marinate for a few hours or preferably overnight.

2. When ready to cook, coarsely crush the cassia, cardamom pods, cloves and peppercorns together using a mortar and pestle. Place a large heavy-based saucepan over a medium heat. When hot, add the oil along with the butter. Add the crushed cassia mixture and let it sizzle for a few seconds to infuse the oil. Now add the onions and fry for 18–20 minutes, stirring often. Add the slit chillies and stir. When the onions start to soften and turn dark brown, add the chilli powder, turmeric, ground coriander and tomato purée. Fry for a minute, stirring to make sure the spice mix doesn't stick to the bottom of the pan.

3. Tip in the marinated lamb shanks and cook for 7–10 minutes, stirring well. This might be a bit tricky, but just keep them moving in the pan and sealing evenly. Take the saucepan off the heat and stir in the yoghurt a little at a time. Put the pan back on the heat, add 400ml water and stir well to make a creamy gravy. Season to taste.

4. Bring the curry to a boil, cover and simmer for 1 hour and 15 minutes, stirring and turning the shanks from time to time until they are cooked through. Add the nutmeg and rose water. Stir well and simmer with the lid slightly open for 20 minutes. The lamb at this stage will be tender and the curry will thicken and go a deep rich colour.

5. Garnish with the coriander and some lemon juice. Serve with roti or naan and a salad.

Malwani Hirwa Tisrya Masala

...CLAMS COOKED IN CORIANDER AND COCONUT

1.6kg clams

2 tbsp vegetable oil

1 red onion (about 80g), finely chopped

4 garlic cloves, finely chopped

2.5cm piece of fresh root ginger, finely chopped

¼ tsp ground turmeric

1 tsp Kashmiri chilli powder or mild paprika

½ tsp garam masala

2 heaped tsp tamarind paste

salt to taste

2 tbsp finely chopped fresh coriander to garnish

FOR THE COCONUT PASTE

2 tbsp vegetable oil

2 red onions (about 160g total weight), thinly sliced

150g freshly grated coconut

50g desiccated coconut

60g fresh coriander leaves and stems

2 green bird's eye chillies (or more if you like it spicy)

In this recipe, tisrya (coastal clams) are cooked in a coconut gravy and a ground paste made from coriander, garlic and pepper. The thick masala coats the clams as they cook in their own stock.

1. Put the clams in a large saucepan with 400ml of warm water. Bring to a boil and simmer for 3–4 minutes or until the shells have opened. Discard any that are unopened after 5 minutes. Strain the cooking liquid through a fine sieve or muslin to get rid of any grit, and reserve 200ml of the liquid.

2. Now make the coconut paste. Place a large frying pan over a low heat and add the oil. When hot, add the onions and fry for 8–10 minutes on a low heat. As they soften and turn light brown, add the fresh and desiccated coconut. Fry for a further 4–5 minutes until they dry out slightly and go a pale brown colour, then add the coriander and bird's eye chillies and fry for 2 minutes. Leave the mixture to cool slightly, then blend with 250ml water to form a thick paste. Set the paste aside while you make the tisrya masala.

3. Place a large heavy-based saucepan over a medium heat and add the first amount of oil. When hot, add the chopped onion and fry for 6 minutes until it starts to go brown. Add the chopped garlic and ginger and fry for 20 seconds, stirring well to make sure the mixture doesn't stick to the bottom of the pan.

4. Add the coconut paste along with the turmeric, chilli powder and garam masala and fry for 3–4 minutes. Again, stir well, scraping the bottom of the pan if it sticks. Add the tamarind paste, 200ml cooking liquid and salt, stir well and simmer over a low heat for a minute. The gravy should be thick so that it coats the clams and also helps them absorb all the flavour.

Continued opposite

5. Now add the opened and cleaned clams and stir well to make sure the masala coats them all. (This will require some armwork!) Cover and simmer over a low heat for 5–7 minutes until the clams are cooked, stirring from time to time to make sure they remain well coated in the masala.

6. Garnish with plenty of coriander and serve warm with chapattis and salad.

TIP
· · · · · ·
Make sure to buy clams that are undamaged and shut. If any are open, tap lightly and discard those that fail to close. Remember that clams like to burrow in the sand, so they must be washed before use to get rid of any grittiness.

Photograph overleaf

Laal Maas...RAJASTHANI LAMB CURRY

850g leg of lamb on the bone, cut into bite-sized chunks (ask your butcher to do this)
16 dried Kashmiri chillies
200ml warm water
8 garlic cloves
3 tbsp vegetable oil
8 green cardamom pods
2 bay leaves
5 cloves
1 onion (about 250g), finely chopped
salt to taste

FOR THE MARINADE
3 tbsp Greek yoghurt
1 heaped tsp Kashmiri chilli powder or mild paprika
2 tsp ground coriander
1 tsp ground cumin

FOR THE GARNISH
chopped fresh coriander
juice of ½ lemon

Traditionally a hot curry, this is a slow-cooked hunter-style lamb dish that uses whole spices to create rustic flavours. I've gone easy on the number of chillies included to tone down the heat level, but if you like things spicy, I would suggest adding a bit more chilli powder to the lamb marinade. Kashmiri chillies are akin to the Rajasthani Mathania variety, the type traditionally used, in that they lend lovely colour, heat and depth to the curry.

1. First make the marinade. Put the yoghurt and the rest of the marinade ingredients in a bowl and stir well. Add the lamb pieces, making sure to coat the meat thoroughly in the marinade. Set aside for 2–3 hours or preferably overnight.

2. When ready to cook, deseed the Kashmiri dried chillies and soak in the warm water for about 20 minutes. Measure 70ml of the soaking liquid into a blender, keeping the rest for later. Add half the soaked chillies and the garlic and blitz to a smooth paste. Transfer to a bowl. Blitz the remaining chillies separately to a coarse paste with 50ml of the reserved soaking liquid and set aside in a separate bowl. Save any remaining soaking liquid to add to the curry later.

3. Place a heavy-based wide saucepan over a medium heat and add the oil. When hot add the cardamom pods, bay leaves and cloves and fry for 20 seconds, allowing them to sizzle and infuse the oil. Add the onion and fry for 8–10 minutes until it starts to change colour and soften. Add the smooth chilli-garlic paste and stir through, cooking for about 2 minutes.

Continued opposite

4. Now add all the lamb along with its marinade.
Turn the heat up slightly and fry for 7–8 minutes,
allowing the meat to seal and soak in the flavour
of the chilli gravy. Pour in 180ml water along
with any remaining chilli soaking liquid and
season to taste. Stir well and bring to a boil,
then turn down the heat, cover and simmer gently
for 1 hour, until the meat is tender and falling
off the bone. Stir the curry halfway through
cooking and add the remaining coarse chilli paste
and a splash of water if required. The gravy
should reduce and have a thick consistency.

5. Garnish with the coriander and lemon juice.
Serve warm with your choice of bread and a cooling
raita.

TIP
......
Kashmiri chillies, which are dried whole, are widely
sold in shops and online. Wherever recipes suggest
the use of 'dried mild chillies', I recommend using
Kashmiri ones. When fried in oil, they lend a deep,
smoky flavour to the dish. When used in marinades or
as part of a spice paste, they must be soaked first
in warm water, then blitzed to a smooth paste, as in
the recipe above. In this way they not only impart a
vibrant colour, but also thicken the curry.

Maharashtrian Green Pea Usal
...GREEN PEA, CORIANDER AND COCONUT CURRY

2 tbsp vegetable oil

pinch of asafoetida

1 tsp cumin seeds

1 tsp Kashmiri chilli powder or mild paprika

400g frozen green peas

2 tsp jaggery or sugar

salt to taste

chopped fresh coriander to garnish

FOR THE PASTE

40g fresh coriander

50g freshly grated coconut, or desiccated coconut soaked for 2 minutes in warm water and drained

5 garlic cloves

1 red onion (about 30g), roughly chopped

juice of 1 lime

Here's a little gem of a vegetarian offering from my household. This green pea curry, commonly called usal, is sweet, spicy and tangy all at once.

1. First make the paste. Put all the ingredients for it into a blender, add 50ml water and blitz.

2. Place a heavy-based saucepan over a medium heat and add the oil. When hot, add the asafoetida and cumin seeds and let them sizzle for a few seconds to infuse the oil. Add the ground paste and fry for 2—3 minutes, stirring to make sure it doesn't stick to the bottom of the pan. Add the chilli powder and fry for a further minute, then add the green peas and mix well for a minute. Add 250ml water, the jaggery and salt, mixing well to form a thick gravy.

3. Bring to a boil, cover and simmer for 5—7 minutes, then remove from the heat and garnish with the coriander. Serve warm with chapattis.

Parsi Mutton Pulao

700g lamb on the bone, cut into bite-sized pieces

1 tbsp yoghurt

1 heaped tbsp garlic and ginger paste (made from 8 garlic cloves and a 5cm piece of fresh root ginger)

pinch of salt

3 tbsp vegetable oil

1 onion (about 240g), thinly sliced

1 potato (about 250g), cut in chunks

1 tbsp melted butter

salt to taste

FOR THE SPICE POWDER

6 Kashmiri dried chillies (or other mild dried red chillies)

1 blade of mace

1 star anise

6 cloves

5cm cassia bark

½ tsp ground nutmeg

1 tsp black peppercorns

1 black cardamom pod, seeds only

This is an age-old recipe for a Parsi pulao that is served with dal at Indian weddings. Traditionally, mutton or goat meat is infused with pepper, saffron, cloves and cassia, then slow-cooked. Here I've replaced the goat meat with lamb, which is equally delicious and soaks in all the flavours before the rice is layered over it.

1. Put the lamb in a large mixing bowl. Add the yoghurt, garlic and ginger paste and salt and mix well. Leave to marinate for 2–3 hours or preferably overnight.

2. Grind all the spice powder ingredients in a coffee or spice grinder and set aside.

3. Place a heavy-based saucepan over a medium heat and add 2 tablespoons of the oil. When hot, add the sliced onion and fry for 15–17 minutes until it starts to soften and change colour. Add the spice powder mix and stir for a few seconds before adding the marinated lamb.

4. Cook the lamb on a medium to high heat for 7–8 minutes, stirring well so that the meat seals and is coated with all the spices. Add 100ml water, season to taste and stir well, bringing the curry to a boil. Turn down the heat, cover and simmer for 50 minutes or until the lamb is cooked through, stirring occassionally to ensure it doesn't stick to the bottom of the pan. When it's done, remove from the heat and keep warm. Season to taste.

5. Preheat the oven to 180°C/350°F/Gas mark 4.

6. Place the potato chunks on a baking tray with the remaining tablespoon of oil and a pinch of salt. Roast in the preheated oven for 15 minutes until the edges begin to brown. Cover the baking tray with foil and set aside in a warm place ready to assemble the pulao.

Continued opposite

FOR THE RICE

pinch of saffron
3 cloves
1 bay leaf
4 green cardamom pods
500g basmati rice
½ tsp butter

TO FINISH THE PULAO

3 tbsp vegetable oil
2 red onions (about 230g total weight), thinly sliced
pinch of sugar
1 tbsp cashew nuts roughly chopped
1 tbsp raisins
2 hard-boiled eggs, quartered
roughly chopped fresh coriander to garnish

7. Now start preparing the rice by soaking the saffron in a small bowl with 2 tablespoons warm water for about 10 minutes.

8. Put 1.5 litres water in a large saucepan and bring to a rolling boil. Add the cloves, bay leaf, cardamom pods and a pinch of salt, stir well, then add the rice and butter. Bring to a boil over a medium heat and cook the rice for 16—18 minutes until three-quarters done (cooked on the outside with a slight bite in the middle) and most of the water has been absorbed. Drain any leftover water and then transfer half the rice to a bowl and pour in the saffron and its soaking water. Stir well so it becomes golden yellow.

9. Working quickly, pour half the melted butter into a deep casserole dish. Cover the base with a layer of white rice, then a layer of the cooked lamb and its sauce, followed by a few roasted potato chunks, then a layer of the saffron rice. Repeat these layers, finishing with a layer of the rice. Pour over the remaining melted butter. Cover the dish with greaseproof paper or foil and a tight-fitting lid and place in the oven for 25 minutes. The rice should be fluffy and the lamb moist and succulent. Once done, leave the pulao to rest while you get the final ingredients ready.

10. To finish the pulao, place a frying pan over a medium heat and add 1 tablespoon of the oil. When hot, add the onions and sugar and fry for 8—10 minutes. When the onions change colour and go brown, transfer them to a bowl. Add the remaining oil to the pan and fry the cashews and raisins for about a minute, stirring continuously, until the nuts start to roast and the raisins swell.

11. Fluff up the pulao lightly with a fork and serve on a platter topped with the fried onions, cashew nuts, raisins and boiled eggs.

12. Garnish with the coriander and serve with dal or even a raita.

Murgh Makhani...BUTTER CHICKEN

FOR THE TANDOORI CHICKEN

2.5cm piece of fresh root ginger

4 garlic cloves

1 green bird's eye chilli

2 tbsp Greek yoghurt

2 tsp gram (chickpea) flour

1 tsp mild paprika

½ tsp Kashmiri chilli powder (or a little more if you'd like it spicy)

½ tsp garam masala

1 tsp ground coriander

pinch of ground cinnamon

pinch of crushed saffron

450g skinless boneless chicken thighs, cut into bite-sized pieces

salt to taste

butter for basting

1 tsp chaat masala

juice of ½ lemon

salad and chutney to serve

This was recently voted in a survey as one of people's top ten dishes to eat on their bucket list! Don't let the list of ingredients or the length of the recipe put you off making it. As soon as you take your first mouthful, you'll know why it made that list. Murgh Makhani — which is basically tandoori chicken in a buttery sauce — is an all-time Indian favourite and one of the dishes we always used to order when we visited restaurant as kids. With those childhood tastes lingering in my memory, I always yearned to recreate that authentic flavour, and nothing delights me more than when people who have tried this recipe come back saying it's the best dish they have ever eaten.

TANDOORI CHICKEN...

1. Put 5-6 wooden skewers in water and leave them to soak.

2. Put the ginger, garlic and bird's eye chilli into a wet grinder or mini food processor and blitz to a smooth paste. Set aside.

3. Put the yoghurt in a bowl. Add the gram flour and mix well to get rid of any lumps and create a thick, paste-like consistency. Add the ginger-garlic paste, the paprika, chilli powder, garam masala, coriander, cinnamon, saffron and salt. Stir well, then add the chicken, mixing well to make sure the pieces are coated in the thick marinade. Leave to marinate for 2-3 hours or preferably overnight.

4. When ready to cook, preheat the grill until medium-hot.

Continued overleaf

FOR THE MURGH MAKHANI GRAVY

1½ tbsp unsalted butter

6 green cardamom pods, lightly crushed

2.5cm cassia bark

4 cloves

1 onion (about 50g), finely chopped

1 heaped tbsp grated ginger (made from a 8cm piece of fresh root ginger)

2 green bird's eye chillies, slit lengthways

1 tsp Kashmiri chilli powder or mild paprika

½ tsp garam masala

3 tbsp tomato purée

150ml double cream

2 tbsp honey

1 tbsp kasoori methi (dried fenugreek leaf)

salt to taste

chopped fresh coriander to garnish

TIP
• • •
Crush the dried fenugreek with your fingers before adding to release the aromas in the curry.

5. Shake the excess marinade off the chicken pieces and thread them onto the skewers. Place them on a wire rack and grill on the top shelf for 15–20 minutes, turning the skewers every 5 minutes and basting with melted butter until the meat juices run clear. The chicken should be cooked through and slightly charred around the edges.

6. If you wish, the tandoori chicken can be served at this point just as it is — over roti or parathas sprinkled with chaat masala and lemon juice, along with a salad and Mint and Coriander Chutney (see page 225). However, to make authentic butter chicken, serve with the gravy below.

MURGH MAKHANI GRAVY...

1. Place a deep saucepan over a low heat and add the butter. When hot, add the cardamom pods, cassia bark and cloves. Fry for 20 seconds, then add the onion and sauté for 5–7 minutes over a medium heat until it takes on a light brown colour.

2. Add the grated ginger and bird's eye chillies. Fry for a further minute, add the chilli powder and garam masala, stir for 20 seconds and add the tomato purée. Mix well and cook for a couple of minutes. Now gradually add the double cream, stirring continuously to mix it with all the spices. Simmer for 2 minutes. Stir in the honey and fenugreek. Season to taste and add 50ml water.

3. Add the cooked chicken pieces and simmer the curry over a low heat for 6–8 minutes.

4. Garnish with coriander and serve with naan bread.

Saag Gosht...MUGHLAI LAMB AND SPINACH CURRY

850g leg of lamb on the bone, cut into bite-sized pieces (ask your butcher to do this)

1 heaped tbsp ginger and garlic paste (made from 8 garlic cloves and a 4cm piece of fresh root ginger)

2 tbsp vegetable oil

3 onions (about 380g total weight), thinly sliced

pinch of sugar

2 tomatoes (about 200g total weight), roughly chopped

350g spinach leaves

2 green bird's eye chillies

2 tbsp mustard oil

½ tsp mild chilli powder

½ tsp ground cumin

1 tsp ground coriander

salt to taste

1.5cm piece of fresh root ginger, cut into slivers, to garnish

Saag Ghost (lamb with spinach) is synonymous with Mughal cooking and is traditionally quite a rich dish. This recipe is adapted from various versions I have cooked and eaten over the years. Some families swear by using mustard oil instead of regular vegetable oil, and it's true, the pungent flavour of mustard oil works very well with the thick rich curry, but if you can't get hold of any, using vegetable oil would be perfectly fine.

1. Put the lamb into a bowl and add half the ginger-garlic paste. Mix well and leave to marinate for 2–3 hours or preferably overnight.

2. When ready to cook, place a frying pan over a medium heat and add the oil. When hot, add the sliced onions and sugar, mix well and fry for 15–17 minutes until the onions soften and go dark brown. Drain on kitchen paper. Leave to cool, then place in a blender with the tomatoes and 50ml water and blitz to a thick, fine purée. Transfer to a bowl and set aside.

3. Reserve a handful of spinach leaves and put the rest in the empty blender. Add the bird's eye chillies and 40ml water and blitz to a purée. Chop the reserved spinach and mix it with the purée, ready to add to the curry when required.

4. Now make the masala. Place a heavy-based saucepan over a medium heat and add the mustard oil. When hot, add the onion-tomato paste and fry for 6–7 minutes. Add the remaining ginger-garlic paste and fry for a further 2 minutes. Stir in the chilli powder, cumin and coriander, then add the marinated lamb and turn up the heat ever so slightly. Fry for 4–5 minutes, sealing the meat and coating the pieces with the masala.

5. Add 100ml water, bring to a boil and simmer, covered, for 45 minutes. Add the spinach purée and season to taste. Continue simmering for a further 30 minutes, stirring a few times to make sure the curry doesn't stick to the bottom of the pan.

6. Garnish with slivers of ginger and serve with chapattis or Simple Pulao (see page 235).

Ragda Patties...POTATO CAKES WITH TANGY CHICKPEA STEW

MAKES 10–12

slice of white bread

500g potatoes, boiled and mashed

1 tsp ginger paste (2.5cm piece of fresh root ginger)

½ tsp green chilli paste (see Tip)

pinch of sugar

1 tsp lemon juice

1 tbsp chopped fresh coriander

2 tsp cornflour

2 tbsp vegetable oil

FOR THE RAGDA

500g canned chickpeas, drained

2 tbsp vegetable oil

1½ tsp black/brown mustard seeds

¼ tsp asafoetida

1 onion (about 100g), finely chopped

8–10 fresh curry leaves

200g tomatoes, finely chopped

½ tsp ground turmeric

½ tsp Kashmiri chilli powder or mild paprika

2 tsp tamarind paste

2 tsp sugar

½ tsp garam masala

lemon juice to taste

salt to taste

chopped fresh coriander

A traditional ragda gravy is made with safed vatana (dried white peas), a yellowish-white legume available from Asian grocers and online. They need to be soaked overnight and then cooked down really well to give a starchy consistency so that the ragda is hearty and comforting. As they take quite a while to cook, I use a pressure cooker to speed things up, or — as here — use chickpeas instead!

1. First make the Ragda gravy. Put the chickpeas in a large pan with enough water to cover and boil over a low heat for 20 minutes or until soft when pressed between your fingers. (Canned chickpeas can vary in quality, so cook for a little longer if necessary.)

2. Place a heavy-based saucepan over a medium heat and add the oil. When hot, add the mustard seeds and asafoetida and allow the seeds to splutter. Add the onion and fry for about 7 minutes until softened, then lower the heat and add the curry leaves, frying for 20 seconds. Add the chopped tomatoes, cooking and stirring for only 2–3 minutes.

3. When the chickpeas are ready, drain them, reserving 300ml of the cooking liquid. Add the chickpeas to the onion mixture, then stir in the turmeric, chilli powder, tamarind paste and sugar. Stir well for about a minute to make sure the spices mix through the chickpeas, and to allow the raw flavours of the spices to cook out. Add the reserved cooking water and mix well (the curry should have a gravy-like consistency but still be slightly thick). Cover and simmer for 20–25 minutes, stirring halfway through cooking. Mash a few of the chickpeas with the back of the spoon to help thicken the curry.

4. Meanwhile, make the patties. Soak the slice of bread in a tiny bit of water for a couple of seconds and squeeze out any excess moisture. Put the bread in a bowl and add the mashed potato, some salt, the ginger and chilli pastes, mixing well with the sugar, lemon juice, coriander and cornflour. Mix well and shape into 10–12 little

Continued opposite

TO SERVE

1 red onion (about 80g), finely chopped

juice of 1 lemon

3 tbsp chopped fresh coriander

Mint and Coriander Chutney (see page 225)

Tamarind Chutney (see page 222)

4–5 tbsp natural yoghurt, whisked with 20ml water

patties around 4cm in diameter. Leave in the refrigerator for 15 minutes to firm up.

5. Heat the oil in a frying pan and fry the patties for 2–3 minutes on each side until golden brown and crisp.

6. Turn off the heat under the ragda, and add the garam masala along with some lemon juice and salt to taste. Stir through and garnish with coriander.

7. To serve, place 2 patties in a bowl and top with a generous portion of the ragda gravy. Sprinkle with some chopped onion, lemon juice and coriander, and put a generous helping of the chutneys and yoghurt alongside.

TIP
......
While it's best to make ginger paste yourself by pounding fresh ginger, it's fine to use shop-bought green chilli paste in this recipe.

Photograph overleaf

Yakhni Pulao

1 onion (about 80g),
roughly chopped

2 bay leaves

5 green cardamom pods

5cm cassia bark

4—5 cloves

1 heaped tsp fennel
seeds

600g shoulder of lamb
on the bone, cut into
medium-sized pieces
(ask your butcher to
do this)

chopped fresh
coriander to garnish

FOR THE PULAO
350g basmati rice

2 tbsp melted butter

2 tbsp vegetable oil

2 bay leaves

2.5cm cassia bark,
broken in half

5 green cardamom pods

2 onions (about 150g
total weight), thinly
sliced

1 heaped tbsp ginger
paste

2 heaped tbsp garlic
paste

2 green bird's eye
chillies, slit
lengthways

1 tsp ground nutmeg

1 tsp ground cinnamon

salt to taste

A celebratory dish that's rich, tasty and lightly spiced, and makes an ideal dinner-party option. The lamb is cooked in whole spices and onions, and the rice is fried with garlic, then cooked with the lamb stock and butter to make for a moist pulao with succulent lamb pieces. Yakhni Pulao is a slow-cooked dish, but when you taste it, you'll know it was time well spent.

1. Put the onion and all the whole spices in a square of muslin, securing it with a string. Put the meat in a stockpot and add about a litre of water (or enough to cover the meat). Add the muslin spice bag and bring to a boil. Lower the heat and simmer for 1 hour 15 minutes. (If you have time, resting the mixture in the pot overnight will enhance the flavours.)

2. When ready to cook, discard the muslin spice bag. Separate the meat and reserve 600ml of the stock. Set both meat and stock aside.

3. To make the pulao, soak the rice for at least 30 minutes, then rinse in a sieve until the water runs clear.

4. Place a heavy-based pan over a medium heat and add the butter and oil. When hot, add the bay leaves, cassia bark and cardamom pods and fry them for a minute as they sizzle and release their flavours into the oil. Add the sliced onions and fry over a medium heat for 7—8 minutes or until they soften and are a light golden brown colour.

5. Add the ginger and garlic pastes along with the chillies and cook through for a couple of minutes. Now add the nutmeg and cinnamon, stirring well for a few seconds to make sure they don't burn. Mix in the cooked lamb and the rice. Season with salt, then add the reserved stock and mix well. Cover and cook over a low heat for about 20 minutes or so until the rice is completely cooked and the liquid has been absorbed.

6. Remove from the heat and garnish with fresh coriander. Serve warm with mint raita.

Khajoor ka Halwa...WARM DATE PUDDING

5–6 walnuts, broken into pieces
30g butter
270g soft dates (see Tip), pitted and roughly chopped
200ml full-fat milk
100ml condensed milk
½ tsp freshly ground cardamom
¼ tsp ground nutmeg
handful of chopped pistachios to garnish

A warm north Indian date pudding made with rich milk, spices, walnuts and butter or ghee.

1. Place a dry pan over a low heat. Add the walnuts and dry-roast them for 3–4 minutes until lightly coloured and crunchy. Leave them to cool slightly, then roughly crush them.

2. Place a small saucepan over a low heat and add the butter. When hot, add the dates and fry for a couple of minutes. Add the full-fat and condensed milks, stir well and simmer for 5 minutes. Mash the dates slightly with the back of a spoon, and stir from time to time, adding a little more milk if the mixture is too thick.

3. Add the cardamom and nutmeg and continue to simmer for a further minute until the halwa has a creamy texture.

4. Remove from the heat and add the walnuts, stirring through. Serve the halwa warm, garnished with chopped pistachios.

TIP
......
I recommend using Medjool dates because they are both soft and sweet. I also advise using freshly ground cardamom and nutmeg, which have a much better flavour than the ready-ground varieties.

Gharge...SPICED PUMPKIN PANCAKES

MAKES 8-10 SMALL PANCAKES

8 green cardamom pods, seeds only

150g canned pumpkin purée

120g dark jaggery or dark brown sugar

100g chapatti flour

2 tsp coarse semolina

1–2 tbsp oil

oil for deep-frying

salt to taste

TIP
• • • • • •

Gharge keep for up to a week in an airtight container. Just warm them in the oven before eating.

These traditional Indian pumpkin and cardamom-spiced pancakes are cooked with dark brown sugar and deep-fried. Could there be anything more decadent and celebratory?

1. Pound the cardamom seeds to a powder in a spice grinder or using a pestle and mortar. Set aside.

2. Place a small saucepan over a low heat. Add the pumpkin purée, jaggery and a pinch of salt and heat, stirring continuously, for 25 minutes until the mixture is slightly dried out. Leave to cool.

3. Put the flour, semolina and ground cardamom in a mixing bowl. Add the pumpkin purée mixture and 1 tablespoon oil. Mix well and knead to a smooth dough with greased hands (this mixture doesn't need any water). Cover with cling film and leave to rest in the bowl for 10 minutes.

4. Heat a deep-fat fryer to 170°C or fill a large saucepan or kadhai (deep wok) one-third full of oil and heat until a cube of bread dropped into the hot oil sizzles and turns golden brown in 30 seconds.

5. Divide the dough into 8–10 equal portions. Dust a flat work surface with flour and roll out each piece of dough into a disc around 7cm in diameter. Deep-fry until golden brown. Drain on kitchen paper.

6. Serve topped with ice cream and chopped pistachios. A perfect treat!

Bengali Bhapa Doi...STRAWBERRY AND
CARDAMOM YOGHURT PUDDING

MAKES 6 PORTIONS

300g Greek yoghurt

225ml condensed milk

70ml strawberry
purée, plus 5–6 tsbp
extra to garnish

½ tsp ground cardamom

4–6 sliced fresh
strawberries to
garnish

This traditional Bengali yoghurt dessert,
which combines the sweetness of condensed milk
and fruit purée with crushed cardamom, is made
in clay pots, then set after being steamed.
It's best served chilled and is a great choice
when you need to make a dessert in advance.

1. Preheat the oven to 140°C/275°F/Gas mark 1. Line
the base of six 85ml ramekins with baking paper and
set aside.

2. Put the yoghurt and condensed milk into a bowl
and whisk together until smooth. Add the berry
purée and the cardamom. Divide the mixture between
the ramekins.

3. Put the lined ramekins in a roasting tin and
pour in enough water to come a quarter of the way
up the side of the dishes. Place in the oven for
35 minutes until firm. Leave the puddings to cool,
then refrigerate them overnight to set fully.

4. To serve, turn out the Bhapa Doi onto serving
plates and top with the fresh strawberry slices and
the extra purée.

EXTRAS

Pineapple and Black Pepper Chutney

4 tbsp mustard or vegetable oil

1 heaped tsp cumin seeds, coarsely ground

3 garlic cloves, finely chopped

2.5cm piece of fresh root ginger, finely chopped

1.5kg canned pineapple chunks, drained and chopped

220g dark brown sugar

40ml malt vinegar

1 heaped tbsp black peppercorns, coarsely ground

One of my favourite chutneys to make, and over the years it's been an absolute crowd pleaser — if you're looking to win brownie points at your dinner party, this is definitely one to serve! I prefer canned pineapple to fresh as it's chopped (saving time) and also much sweeter than the fruit in its natural state (but do make sure to drain off any liquid).

1. Place a large heavy-based saucepan over a high heat and add the oil. If using mustard oil, heat to smoking point, then cool and leave to rest for 3–4 minutes before reheating over a low heat. If using vegetable oil, just heat in the usual way.

2. Add the cumin seeds and fry for a few seconds, followed by the garlic and ginger. Fry for a couple of minutes, then add the pineapple chunks and stir well, cooking on a medium heat for 10 minutes. Now add the sugar and vinegar, stirring well to make sure the sugar has dissolved. Add most of the black pepper, leaving a little behind.

3. Simmer the chutney over a low heat, cooking gently, without a lid, for 1 hour 45 minutes. Stir occasionally to make sure it doesn't stick to the bottom of the pan. (Pineapple is naturally juicy, so this chutney doesn't require any water, but if you feel it is drying out slightly, you can add a few tablespoons of water at this stage and simmer.) As the moisture evaporates, the chutney will become syrupy and darken. Now add the remaining black pepper and stir well.

4. Leave to cool, then decant into sterilised jars (see Tip). Seal and leave unopened in a cool place for 3–4 days before using. The chutney will keep refrigerated for 4 weeks.

TIP

To sterilise jars, wash them thoroughly in hot soapy water, rinse well, then put them on a baking tray and place in an oven preheated to 100°C/200°F/Gas mark 2. Gently heat through for at least 15 minutes.

Bengali Spiced Grape Chutney

2 tbsp vegetable oil

1 tbsp panch puran spice mix

1 dried mild chilli, halved

2.5 cm piece of fresh root ginger, finely grated

800g red seedless grapes

2 tbsp lemon juice

80g dark brown sugar

pinch of chilli flakes

With its inclusion of panch puran, this chutney, made from slowly cooked grapes, has distinct east Indian influences. Given its sweetness, it is best accompanied by spicy dishes, and is perfect as part of a feast alongside pulaos or rich curries.

1. Place a heavy-based saucepan over a medium heat and add the oil. When hot, add the panch puran spice mix and let it sizzle for 10 seconds to infuse the oil.

2. Add the chilli and ginger and fry for a few seconds, then quickly add the grapes. Stir well and add the lemon juice along with the sugar. Mix well, then add 100ml water. Bring to a boil and simmer over a low heat, cooking for 1 hour 40 minutes without a lid, stirring occasionally until the mixture is sticky and slightly runny (it will thicken as it cools). Finally, add the chilli flakes and mix well.

3. Decant the chutney into a sterilised jar (see Tip, page 218), refrigerate and use within a week.

Sticky Sweet Chilli Dipping Sauce

1 tbsp vegetable oil
½ tsp cumin seeds
½ tsp mild Kashmiri chilli powder or mild paprika
120g caster sugar
pinch of salt

A dipping sauce that's perfect with snacks and light bites, such as Bengali Prawn Cakes (page 132) or Haraa Paneer Tikkas (page 92).

1. Place a small saucepan over a low heat and add the oil. When hot, add the cumin seeds and fry for just a few seconds. Add the chilli powder, stir for 5 seconds, then add 70ml water, the sugar and a pinch of salt. Stir well, making sure to dissolve the sugar completely.

2. Simmer for 3—4 minutes over a low heat, then leave to cool slightly (the sauce will thicken as it does so). Use straight away.

Tamarind Chutney

45g tamarind paste
90g light brown sugar
¼ tsp ground ginger
¼ tsp mild chilli powder
¼ tsp cumin seeds, coarsely crushed
pinch of salt

A fresh, tangy chutney in which the hint of sweetness provided by the sugar is perfectly balanced by the savoury notes of ground ginger and chilli powder. This is a versatile chutney, which can be served with snacks, sandwiches or even as part of a main meal.

Blitz all the ingredients together in a blender with 50ml water. The chutney should be runny, with a pouring consistency. If you prefer it thicker, add a little less water. Decant the chutney into a bowl, refrigerate and use within a week.

Aubergine Pickle

200ml mustard or
vegetable oil

2 heaped tsp cumin
seeds

1 tsp black mustard
seeds

1 tsp fenugreek seeds

1½ tsp mild chilli
powder

2 aubergines (about
450g total weight),
diced into small
cubes

140ml malt vinegar

3 tbsp caster sugar

1 tsp salt

FOR THE PASTE

15 garlic cloves,
roughly chopped

5 cm piece of fresh
root ginger, roughly
chopped

2 small green bird's
eye chillies

2 tsp coriander seeds

2 tsp sesame seeds

2–3 tbsp malt vinegar

TIP
• • • • • •

However strongly you
may be tempted, never
add water to this
while cooking — it
will last longer if
you don't.

One of my favourite pickles — I remember that
when my mother served it out I could have
eaten it just on its own with plain rice or
chapattis. The recipe is very forgiving —
all you need to remember is that the flavours
should be balanced out. The imperative
ingredient in most Indian pickles is mustard
oil, which does add the pungency you need,
but you can replace it here with vegetable
oil if mustard oil isn't available.

1. First make the paste. Put all the ingredients
for it in a blender and blitz to a smooth paste.
Set aside.

2. Place a heavy-based saucepan over a medium
heat and add the oil. When hot, add the cumin and
mustard seeds. As they begin to splutter, add the
fenugreek seeds and fry for 5 seconds. Now add the
paste and fry on a medium heat for 5–6 minutes.
Stir well.

3. Add the chilli powder, aubergines, vinegar,
sugar and salt. Bring to a boil and simmer on a
low heat for 30 minutes without the lid. (Keep
stirring every 15 minutes to make sure the mixture
doesn't stick to the bottom of the pan.)

4. Leave to cool, then decant into a sterilised
jar (see page 218). Seal the jar and store for a
week before opening. This pickle will keep for a
few weeks — or maybe just a few days in my case!

Red Chilli Coconut Chutney

150g freshly grated
or desiccated coconut

2 shallots (about
20g total weight),
roughly chopped

1.5cm piece of fresh
root ginger, roughly
chopped

1 garlic clove

2 tsp tamarind paste
(see Tip)

10 fresh curry leaves

salt to taste

FOR THE TADKA

1 tbsp vegetable oil

1 tsp black mustard
seeds

½ tsp Kashmiri chilli
powder or mild
paprika

The vibrant red colour of this chutney comes from the Kashmiri chilli powder, and it's the combination of this with the tamarind, coconut, curry leaves and ginger that makes it so special — definitely one to try! This fresh chutney can be served with snacks or as part of a main meal. I have added only a touch of chilli powder, but feel free to add more if you prefer it a tad spicier.

1. Put the coconut, shallots, ginger, garlic and tamarind into a blender along with 5 curry leaves and some salt. Add 50ml water and blitz to a paste. Pour the chutney mix into a bowl.

2. To make the tadka, place a frying pan over a low heat and add the oil. When hot, add the mustard seeds and, as they begin to splutter, add the chilli powder then turn off the heat.

3. Add the remaining curry leaves, pour the mixture over the chutney and stir. Decant the chutney into a bowl, refrigerate and use within a few days.

TIP
......
Tamarind paste varies in strength, some brands being a lot stronger than others, so add it carefully and keep tasting your chutney until you get the flavour you like.

Mint and Coriander Chutney

40g cashew nuts
20g fresh coriander
leaves
40g fresh mint leaves
1.3cm piece of fresh
root ginger, roughly
chopped
1 small bird's eye
chilli
1 tsp sugar
juice of 1 lime
salt to taste

One of the most popular of all fresh Indian chutneys, and great with recipes such as Bohra-style Fried Lamb Chops, Murghi na Farcha or even the Prawns Rawa Fry (see pages 98, 107 or 33). Nut pastes are a common addition to curries and chutneys across India — they help give a thicker consistency to the dish. I have used cashews here, but you can swap them for roasted peanuts if you prefer.

1. Soak the cashew nuts in warm water for 20–30 minutes, until softened.

2. Transfer the nuts to a blender with a little of their soaking water, add the rest of the ingredients and blitz to a smooth fine paste. Season to taste. Add a little more water to make a slightly runny dipping chutney.

3. Decant the chutney into a bowl, refrigerate and use within a few days.

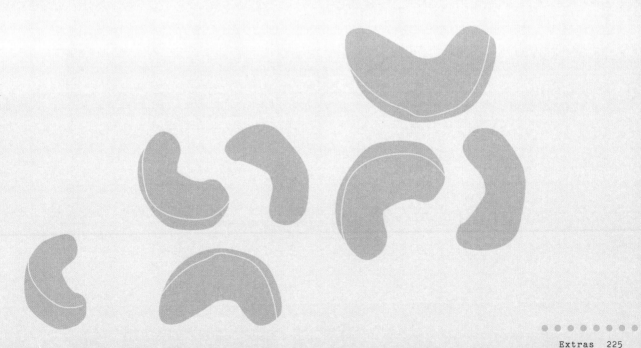

Five-minute Naan Bread

MAKES 4
250g plain flour
1 tsp baking powder
1 tsp sugar
½ tsp salt
90ml full-fat milk
2 tbsp vegetable oil
2 tbsp natural
yoghurt, lightly
whisked
butter for brushing

FOR THE GARNISH
finely chopped fresh
coriander or mint
a sprinkling of
black onion seeds
(optional)

The UK's favourite flatbread with a curry!
I've simplified it with an easy recipe that
doesn't use yeast or need proving, and also
has a really short cooking time.

1. Sift the flour, baking powder, sugar and salt in
a mixing bowl.

2. Mix the milk and oil together in a separate
bowl.

3. Add the yoghurt to the flour followed by the
milk mixture. Stir well to make a soft, pliable
dough. Turn out on the work surface and knead for
a couple of minutes until smooth. Place the dough
back in the bowl, cover with cling film and rest
for 10 minutes in a warm place.

4. Preheat the grill to medium. Line a baking tray
with greaseproof paper and place under the grill
on the top shelf to heat.

5. Turn out the dough and divide into 4 equal
portions. Roll each out quite thinly into an oval
shape, brush with some butter and lightly prick
with a fork to make sure they don't rise. Add a
garnish of your choice and pat down lightly.

6. Place the naan in the hot tray and return to
the grill for 1½ minutes. Brush with butter and
grill for a further 1–2 minutes or until speckled
lightly brown all over. Serve warm, brushed with
more butter.

Puris

MAKES AROUND 20

200g chapatti flour

4 tbsp vegetable oil, plus extra for rolling

oil for deep-frying

salt to taste

These deep-fried little breads are indulgent, more-ish and a real Indian staple. Serve with a simple Aloo ki Sabzi or a Maharashtrian Rassa (see page 90 or 40), or do as Maharashtrians do and eat them alongside a sweet Shrikhand (see page 111).

1. Put the flour in a bowl along with 2 tablespoons oil. Now add 170ml water, a little at a time, mixing with a spoon or your fingers until the mixture starts to come together. Knead well to form a smooth dough. Add 2 more tablespoons of the oil and knead for a further 2 minutes. Cover the bowl with cling film and leave to rest for 10 minutes.

2. Divide the dough into about 20 equal portions. Dab a little oil on each puri (to help with the rolling) and roll the dough out into thin discs around 8cm in diameter.

3. Heat a deep-fat fryer to 170°C or fill a large saucepan or kadhai (deep wok) one-third full of oil and heat until a cube of bread dropped into the hot oil sizzles and turns golden brown in 30 seconds.

4. Deep-fry a puri for 1–2 minutes, pressing lightly with a slotted spoon as it turns golden and puffs up. Turn it over and cook for a further minute. Drain on kitchen paper while you cook the remaining puris in the same way.

Plain Buttery Parathas

MAKES AROUND 8
250g chapatti flour,
plus extra for
dusting
3 tbsp vegetable oil
pinch of salt
softened butter for
brushing and frying
(approx 70–80g)

These buttery parathas have no stuffing or spices. The recipe uses regular chapatti flour but it's the multiple layers with the addition of butter that make it so delicious. Serve the flaky parathas with curries, or on their own with pickle.

1. Add the flour to a mixing bowl along with the oil and salt. Now add 160–170ml water a little at a time, mixing with a spoon or your fingers until the mixture starts to come together. Knead well to form a smooth dough. Cover the bowl with cling film and leave to rest for 10 minutes.

2. Divide the dough into 8 equal portions and roll out to discs around 13cm in diameter. Brush a little melted butter over the paratha. Fold in half, brush with a bit more butter and fold in half again. Now, using very little flour to dust, reroll the parathas into discs around 18cm in diameter. Don't worry about the shape!

3. Place a frying pan over a low heat and add ½ teaspoon butter. When hot, add a paratha, press down with a spatlua and fry on a low heat for 1–2 minutes. Brush some butter over the top of the paratha and turn it over, frying for a further 2 minutes until it turns golden and has brown speckles. Flip over again, cooking for a final 30 seconds, pressing lightly.

4. Keep warm, wrapped in a tea towel or foil, while you make the rest of the parathas in the same way.

Chapattis

MAKES AROUND 10

250g chapatti flour, plus extra for dusting

3 tbsp vegetable oil

pinch of salt

melted butter to serve

These soft breads topped with butter or ghee are a classic Indian addition to any meal. Perfect with curries and pickles.

1. Add the flour to a mixing bowl along with the oil and salt. Now add 160—170ml water, a little at a time, mixing with a spoon or your fingers until the mixture starts to come together. Knead well to form a smooth dough. Cover the bowl with cling film and leave to rest for 10 minutes.

2. Divide the dough into 10 equal portions and roll into balls. Flatten each ball, dust with a little flour and roll out as thinly as possible into discs around 15cm in diameter.

3. Heat a griddle pan or dry frying pan over a medium heat. When hot, add a circle of dough and cook for 30 seconds, then turn it over and cook for a further minute. As it begins to puff up, turn and cook for a further 30 seconds, pressing lightly with the back of a spatula. Remove from the heat, brush with a little melted butter and keep warm while you make the rest of the chapattis in the same way.

TIP
......
There are various ways of making roti/chapattis. I normally follow the same method that my grandmother used. Follow the first line in step 3 and cook for 30 seconds on each side. Then with the help of tongs put the chapatti on an open flame and tun a couple of times as it begins to puff up and has speckled brown spots all over. Brush with butter and keep warm while you make the remaining chapattis.

Photograph overleaf

Basic Rice Recipe

MAKES ENOUGH FOR 4 PEOPLE
300g basmati rice
salt to taste

Here's a simple way to cook rice so that it has fluffy, separate grains that will soak in all the flavours of the curries. I like to use good-quality basmati rice, which is a long-grain variety.

1. Rinse the rice 3 times under cold running water to get rid of any excess starch.

2. Bring 600ml water to a boil in a small pan. Add the rice along with the salt, and stir. As it starts to boil, lower the heat to a simmer, cover and cook for 10 minutes. Turn off the heat and let it rest for 5 minutes until all the water has evaporated.

3. Using a fork, fluff up the rice and serve warm.

Curd Rice

1 quantity cooked
rice (see opposite)

200g natural yoghurt,
lightly whisked

2 tbsp vegetable oil

1½ tsp cumin seeds

2 small green bird's
eye chillies, finely
chopped

10 fresh curry leaves

salt to taste

chopped fresh
coriander to garnish

TIP
······

If you're making
this a few hours in
advance, add an extra
couple of tablespoons
of yoghurt to the rice
just before serving.

A staple in our household, curd rice would
be eaten with spiced green beans or even a
Baingan ka Bharta (see page 101). The flavour
of spicy dishes eaten alongside this quite
plain yoghurt rice taste amazing.

1. Leave the cooked rice to cool completely and
season if you haven't done so already. Fork
lightly to loosen the grains and set aside.

2. Put the yoghurt in a bowl and add ½ teaspoon
salt. Add 30ml water to thin the yoghurt slightly,
mix well and set aside.

3. Place a heavy-based pan over a medium heat and
add the oil. When hot, add the cumin seeds and fry
for 10 seconds followed by the bird's eye chillies
and curry leaves. Stir for a few seconds, then add
the cooked rice.

4. With the heat on low, stir the rice for just a
minute to heat it through, making sure it doesn't
stick to the bottom of the pan. Turn off the
heat and add the yoghurt. Stir and garnish with
coriander. Serve straight away with a curry or
pickle of your choice.

Lime and Coriander Rice

1 quantity cooked
rice (see page 232)

1 tbsp vegetable oil

1 green bird's eye
chilli, roughly
chopped

2 tsp lime zest

zest and juice of
½ lime

2 tbsp finely chopped
fresh coriander

salt to taste

Zingy and refreshing, this is the perfect accompaniment to a complex Indian curry. It would be great with an Achari Murgh (see page 133) or even a fish curry.

1. Leave the cooked rice to cool completely and season if you haven't done so already. Fork lightly to loosen the grains and set aside.

2. Place a heavy-based saucepan over a medium heat and add the oil. When hot, add the chopped chilli and fry for a few seconds. Add the rice and heat through, stirring well. Add the lime zest and fresh coriander. Mix well and turn off the heat. Add the lime juice and serve.

Simple Pulao

1 quantity cooked
rice (see page 232)
2 tbsp vegetable oil
1 heaped tsp cumin
seeds
4 cloves
40g cashew nuts,
roughly chopped
½ tsp ground turmeric
70g frozen green peas
salt to taste
chopped fresh
coriander to garnish

One of my favourite ways to cook pulao — the colours are vibrant and the inclusion of cashews gives the rice a nutty flavour. If I am cooking an array of curries for a dinner party, this would be ideal to serve with most dishes. It also works as a quick alternative to a classic biryani.

1. Leave the cooked rice to cool completely and season if you haven't done so already. Fork lightly to loosen the grains, then set aside.

2. Place a wok or kadhai over a medium heat and add the oil. When hot, add the cumin seeds and cloves and stir for a couple of seconds. Add the cashew nuts and fry for 30 seconds. As they begin to brown, add the turmeric and the cold rice.

3. Lower the heat and stir well for 30 seconds. Add the green peas and continue frying for a minute. Season to taste. Turn off the heat and add fresh coriander. Serve warm with a curry of your choice.

Koshimbir

2 cucumbers (about
400g total weight),
coarsely grated

150g carrots,
coarsely grated

30g roasted peanuts

½ tsp cumin seeds,
coarsely crushed

1 tbsp desiccated
coconut

2 tbsp chopped fresh
coriander

¼ tsp mild chilli
powder

pinch of sugar

2 tbsp lime juice

salt to taste

A Maharashtrian recipe and one that is eaten in most households in their 'taat' (thali). Mum would make this just with cucumber, but I prefer to add carrot because of its lovely colour. Chilli, lime, sugar and salt are all vital inclusions for their hot, tangy, sweet and sour flavours.

1. Squeeze out as much water from the cucumbers as possible and set them aside in a mixing bowl.

2. Add the carrots, peanuts, cumin seeds, coconut, coriander and chilli powder. Toss and mix well. Just before serving, add the sugar, lime juice and salt and toss again.

Baingan Raita

½ tsp cumin seeds
250ml natural yoghurt
½ tsp mild chilli powder
2 tbsp vegetable oil
1 tsp black mustard seeds
2 dried red mild chillies
12 fresh curry leaves
½ tsp ground turmeric
1 aubergine (about 200g), diced into cubes
salt to taste
1 tbsp chopped fresh coriander

Indians love adding all kinds of veg to yoghurt to make a wholesome hearty raita. This aubergine variation makes a change from the usual onion/tomato version, and has to be my favourite. Serve it with a lentil curry, potato bhajis and some plain rice, or on its own with Simple Pulao (see page 235).

1. Crush the cumin seeds using a pestle and mortar and set aside.

2. Whisk the yoghurt in a bowl, making sure there are no lumps; add 50ml water to thin it down slightly. Add the crushed cumin, the chilli powder and salt. Stir well and set aside.

3. Place a frying pan over a medium heat and add the oil. When hot, add the mustard seeds and let them pop for 10 seconds. Add the chillies, curry leaves and turmeric, stir for a few seconds, then add the diced aubergine. Stir well and cook over a low heat, covered, for 12–14 minutes. (Make sure to stir halfway through cooking.)

4. Leave the aubergine mixture to cool, then add to the yoghurt. Mix the raita well and garnish with the coriander.

Pineapple Raita

500ml natural yoghurt
250g canned pineapple chunks, drained and chopped
1½ tsp black peppercorns, coarsely ground
1 tbsp sugar
½ tsp cumin seeds, coarsely ground
1 tbsp roughly chopped fresh coriander

Like many of the raitas on my list, this isn't in your typical repertoire — and for good reason when there is such a fantastic variety of raita flavours across India. To most people, pineapple with yoghurt is unthinkable, but here its sweetness, along with the warmth from the black pepper and cumin, makes this so more-ish. Indian households would serve this at dinner parties or alongside an array of curries. It's ideal with Punjabi Kaali Dal and Guntur-style Chicken Stir-fry (see pages 138 and 103).

1. Add the yoghurt to a mixing bowl with a couple of tablespoons of water. Mix well.

2. Add the rest of the ingredients, mixing well. Leave to rest and chill before serving.

Beetroot Pachadi

150g cooked beetroot (shop-bought is fine, but not the ones in vinegar!)

100g natural yoghurt

1 tbsp vegetable oil

½ tsp black mustard seeds

1 dried mild red chilli, halved

10—12 fresh curry leaves

salt to taste

FOR THE PASTE

50g freshly grated or desiccated coconut

2.5cm piece of fresh root ginger, roughly chopped

½ tsp black mustard seeds

A traditional southern Indian recipe made with coconut, ginger and chilli, pachadi can be made with any vegetable. I have chosen beetroot here for its vibrant colour and the spice flavours that complement it.

1. Grate the beetroot into a large bowl. Add the yoghurt, mix well and season to taste.

2. To make the paste, put all the ingredients for it into a blender along with a splash of water and blitz until smooth. Add the paste to the beetroot mix and stir well.

3. Place a frying pan over a medium heat and add the oil. When hot, add the mustard seeds then, as they begin to splutter, turn off the heat and quickly add the red chilli and curry leaves. Add this mixture to the beetroot. Stir well and serve.

Burani Raita

¼ tsp cumin seeds
4 garlic cloves, skin on
1 tsp vegetable oil
250ml natural yoghurt
¼ tsp coarsely ground black pepper
sea salt
1 tbsp finely chopped fresh coriander

Here we have roasted garlic raita with a hint of black pepper and cumin. I roast the garlic in the oven on a low heat, which gives it a slightly charred but sweet flavour. Serve the raita with curries, spicy biryanis or pulaos.

1. Preheat the oven to 170°C/325°F/Gas mark 3.

2. Grind the cumin seeds to a coarse powder.

3. Place the garlic on a piece of kitchen foil with the oil and wrap loosely. Place on a baking tray and roast in the oven for 30 minutes. Leave to cool slightly.

4. Whisk the yoghurt in a bowl with 50ml water, making sure there are no lumps. Add the pepper, crushed cumin and salt and mix well.

5. Squeeze the roasted garlic out of its skin. Place in a mortar with a pinch of sea salt and crush with the pestle. Add this to the raita and mix well.

6. Garnish with the coriander and chill before serving.

Green Apple and Fennel Raita

500ml natural yoghurt

½ tsp cumin seeds, coarsely crushed

1 tsp fennel seeds, coarsely crushed

1.5cm piece fresh root ginger, finely grated

1 tbsp sugar

1 Granny Smith apple (about 180g), coarsely grated

salt to taste

Could there be a better pairing than apple and fennel? Green apples are slightly tart, which works well in this recipe. I crush the fennel coarsely for texture and flavour. This raita is delicious with Murgh kali Mirch or Parsi Prawn Patia (see page 134 or 62).

1. Add the yoghurt to a mixing bowl with a couple of tablespoons of water to thin it out slightly. Add the rest of the ingredients, apart from the apple, and mix well.

2. Grate the apple just before adding it to the raita to prevent it from discolouring. Serve chilled.

Nimbu Pani

MAKES 3-4 SMALL GLASSES
juice of 7 limes
90g caster sugar
½ tsp coarsely ground black pepper
½ tsp rock salt (kala namak) or sea salt

A street-vendor favourite sold in cities all across India, Nimbu Pani — made with Indian lemons, sugar and salt — is the perfect thirst-quencher, though I opt for limes in the West as lemons tend to be a tad too sour.

1. Mix all the ingredients together with 450ml water, making sure to dissolve all the sugar.

2. Chill for at least 20 minutes. Serve topped with crushed ice.

Indian Cold Coffee

3 tsp instant coffee
granules
500ml full-fat milk
2 green cardamom
pods, seeds only
110ml condensed milk

TIP
......
Cold coffee is best
drunk immediately,
although leaving
it to chill in the
fridge will enhance
the flavour from the
cardamom. If it's
refrigerated, make
sure to give it a
quick whizz in the
blender again before
serving so that it's
really frothy!

I'm not really much of a coffee drinker,
but, then again, if it has a hint of spice
and crushed ice and is creamy and frothy,
you really can't fault it. More importantly,
making cold coffee in India conjures up
memories I always remember fondly. There's
not much to this drink apart from regular
instant coffee and some cardamom, but it's
a winner nonetheless.

1. Put the coffee granules into a small bowl and
add 1 tablespoon warm water to dissolve them.

2. Transfer to a blender, add all the remaining
ingredients and whizz to mix well.

3. Pour into glasses filled with crushed ice and
serve straight away.

Panha

generous pinch of
saffron
2—3 tbsp warm water
2 unripe green
mangoes (about 900g
total weight)
7—8 green cardamom
pods, seeds only
150g caster sugar

A traditional drink from the Maharashtrian
community in Mumbai. I urge you to try this
during the summer months. Sour mangoes are
great in this drink, which has a gorgeous
colour because of the inclusion of saffron.
Best served chilled.

1. Put the saffron in a small bowl and pour over
the warm water. Set aside to infuse.

2. Put the green mangoes in a large saucepan and
add enough water to cover them (about a litre).
Bring to a boil, then simmer, half-covered, for
50—55 minutes. Drain and set aside to cool.

3. Peel the mangoes and add the pulp to a blender
along with the cardamom seeds, 1 litre water and
the sugar. Blend until smooth. Check for sweetness
and add a touch more sugar if you wish.

4. Empty into a pouring jug, add the saffron
strands along with their soaking water and mix
well. Chill and serve in glasses.

Adrak Chai

4 green cardamom
pods, seeds only

4cm cassia bark,
broken in half

250ml full-fat milk

½ tsp grated fresh
root ginger

2 strong teabags

100ml warm water

3 tsp sugar

TIP
......
If you find this too
sweet, reduce the
amount of sugar.

There are many versions of chai (Indian tea).
Mine doesn't include a plethora of spices —
just an everyday selection of warming ginger,
cardamom and cassia. The cardinal rule for
'tapri chai' (street-stall chai) is that it
must be strong, milky and sweet. Follow these
rules and you'll be hooked on this local brew.

1. Grind the cardamom seeds and cassia bark in a
coffee or spice grinder (they don't have to be
finely powdered).

2. Heat the milk in a small saucepan and add the
ground spices and grated ginger along with the
teabags. Bring to a boil and simmer for 8 minutes,
stirring frequently.

3. Add the warm water and simmer for a further
5 minutes, stirring continuously to make sure the
mixture doesn't stick to the bottom of the pan.
Add the sugar and mix well. Strain, pour into
small glasses and serve hot.

Garam Masala

2–3cm cassia bark
(around 15g)
½ tbsp green cardamom
pod, seeds only
1 star anise
1 blade of mace
6g cloves (just over
½ tbsp)

Garam masala is a blend of aromatic spice used in Indian cooking. Although the word 'garam' means 'hot' this blend is more about warmth and flavour than heat. Each househould has their own blend with various spices used — mine is an age-old recipe (nearly 60 years old!) and one that always lifts the flavour of a curry when added towards the end of cooking.

1. Place a dry frying pan over a low heat. When hot, add all the spices and dry-fry on a low heat for 3–4 minutes, shaking the pan a few times.

2. Cool the spices and blitz in a coffee grinder. Store in an airtight container.

Goda Masala

20g desiccated
coconut
1 tbsp vegetable oil
30g coriander seeds
1 tbsp cumin seeds
5cm cassia bark,
broken into pieces
2 mild dried red
chillies
2 tbsp sesame seeds
6 cloves
4 bay leaves
½ tsp caraway seeds
½ tsp asafoetida
½ tsp ground turmeric

Goda masala is unique to Maharastra and neighbouring coastal cities in the west of India. Sesame seeds and coconut are key ingredients and it is commonly used in dal, meat dishes and even chicken curries. This blend adds the necessary pungency and warmth to an Indian dish.

1. Place a dry frying pan over a low heat. When hot, add the coconut and dry-fry for 3–4 minutes (keep stirring as the coconut colours and turns a light brown). Empty into a bowl.

2. Add the oil and all the remaining ingredients. Fry for 2–3 minutes on a low heat until the spices begin to change colour and have a roasted aroma. Set aside to cool.

3. Grind in a spice or coffee grinder to a fine powder. Store in an airtight container.

Malwani Masala

12 dried red
chillies, deseeded

½ tsp black
peppercorns

2 tbsp coriander
seeds

1 star anise

6 cloves

½ tsp black mustard
seeds

5cm cassia bark

1 black cardamom pod

¾ tsp caraway seeds

½ tsp cumin seeds

1 tbsp fennel seeds

1 tsp ground nutmeg

½ tsp ground turmeric

A spice mixture that comes from the town of
Malwan in Maharastra. It is used mainly in
coastal dishes.

1. Place a dry frying pan over a low heat and
add all the ingredients except the nutmeg and
turmeric. Dry-fry for 5–7 minutes, stirring
occasionally. Set aside to cool.

2. Grind the roasted spices in a coffee or spice
grinder to a fine powder. Mix in the nutmeg and
turmeric and use as required.

TIP
......

Provided it is stored in an airtight container, the
Malwani Masala will keep for a few months. Don't
forget to add a label with the name and date.

Suppliers

Here's a list of some of the best places to stock up on spices.

SPICES OF INDIA

This site is most definitely the 'one stop shop' for everything Indian, from spices and sweets, to incense sticks. Also the quintessential Indian masala dabba which is a household must have.
www.spicesofindia.co.uk

THE SPICE SHOP

Also a long standing little shop on Portobello Road in London, the aromas of the spices are enough to entice a visit to the shop (one that I frequent often!). With a stock of over 2500 products they have a brilliant range of chillies, paprika and ground/whole spices used for Indian cooking.
www.thespiceshop.co.uk

WORLD OF CHILLIES

An amazing website for chilli lovers.
www.worldofchillies.com

MMM-FOOD

A haven in the heart of Grainger Market (Newcastle upon Tyne) for good quality spices alongside oils, vinegars, chutneys and flour.
www.mmm-food.co.uk

STEENBERGS ORGANIC

A family run establishment with emphasis on providing organic spices and a good range of Fairtrade products.
www.steenbergs.co.uk

THE ASIAN COOKSHOP

With over 3000 spices it's really the go to place for Indian spices. They stock smaller quantities too. Also an array of hard to find whole and ground spices, teas, Thai and Chinese cooking ingredients.
www.theasiancookshop.co.uk

ASIAN SUPERMARKETS

Almost anywhere you go you'll find an Asian supermarket. They're so worth a trip for the fresh herbs, spices, chicken, meat and even a variety of vegetables used in Indian cooking.

Taj Stores: 112 Brick Lane, London, E1 6RL
Banglacity: 86, Brick Lane, London, E1 6RL
Banglatown Cash & Carry: 67-77 Hanbury St, London E1 5JP

Godrej Nature's Basket: Mumbai, Delhi, and beyond
www.naturesbasket.co.in

To sink your teeth into the bustle of the city in Delhi I'd definitely recommend an early morning visit to Khari Baoli, the biggest wholesale spice market.

In Mumbai make your way to Mirchi Galli at Crawford Market. It's the city's very own souk!

Index

ACKNOWLEDGEMENTS...

Anyone who has written a cookbook will know how hard it is to express in words the gratitude you feel towards those who have helped bring this book to life.

Everyone I have met and every experience I've had has always taught me to shine brighter. And with that I want to thank the brilliant team at Hodder & Stoughton for bringing to life part of my work and helping me thrive.

Sarah Hammond — for your amazing support and patience. You have been the captain of this ship from the word go. You have always steered me in the direction that I know instinctively has been my calling and which has led to me producing some of my best work for this my first cookbook.

Sarah Williams and Sophie Hicks — from the outset, your vision and belief in me and the work I do is what will always keep me striving for bigger and better things. Never failing to support me (no matter how crazy my ideas might be!) and telling me how we can make it happen.

Helen Cathcart — for these stunning images and making my food look so very delicious. At times during the book shoot it was all very overwhelming but truly something I will cherish. And to River for his support!

Patrick Budge — this book captures the essence of my cooking and I have you to thank. Your talent in making Indian Kitchen look amazing has floored me.

Lisa Harrison, Jo Harris and Jane Brown — thank you so much for your tireless work through the shoot and taking the time to give feedback. And your kind words of reassurance, Lisa.

Mum and Dad — for instilling in me determination and hard work. Through all our successes, challenges and life experiences to savour every moment and keep going, no matter what.

To all my amazing friends who've supported my work through the years. There are so many of you wonderful people who are part of my life and every step of the way you have encouraged me and I am eternally grateful.

Johann — you are the light and love of Mummy's life. I am so proud of you and all that you bring to our lives. I hope this book is something you will look back on and remember fondly for not just the recipes but also the family connections and memories. I hope you're able to carry this forward with you. Cook, share and do it all with loads of enthusiasm.

And finally Bharat — for being part of this amazing life we live and making fond memories along the way. There would be no Indian Kitchen without you. For being my soul mate, best friend, husband and my biggest supporter through it all. Always encouraging me to go for it and reminding me what my prime focus in life is when I go astray. For the adventures we have and making it fun, thriving in it and living to the fullest. I wouldn't have it any other way, babe.

First published in Great Britain in 2015
by Hodder & Stoughton
An Hachette UK company

1

A CIP catalogue record for this title is available from
the British Library

Hardback ISBN 978 1 444 79455 7
Ebook ISBN 978 1 444 79456 4

Editor SARAH HAMMOND
Copy Editor MIREN LOPATEGUI
Design & Art Direction PATRICK BUDGE
Photographer HELEN CATHCART
Food Stylist LISA HARRISON
Props Stylist JO HARRIS

Typeset in Pica

Printed and bound in China by C&C Offset Printing Co., Ltd.

Hodder & Stoughton policy is to use papers that are
natural, renewable and recyclable products and made
from wood grown in sustainable forests. The logging and
manufacturing processes are expected to conform to the
environmental regulations of the country of origin.

Hodder & Stoughton Ltd
Carmelite House
50 Victoria Embankment
London, EC4Y 0DZ

www.hodder.co.uk